S0-BDT-332

ANTIQUES AND THEIR VALUES

# TABLES

COMPILED BY TONY CURTIS

First Published 1979.

Converted at the rate of exchange on the day of sale.

ISBN 902921-86-X

Published by Lyle Publications, Glenmayne, Galashiels, Selkirkshire, Scotland.
Distributed in the U.S.A. by Apollo, 391 South Road, Poughkeepsie, N.Y. 12601.

# INTRODUCTION

Congratulations! You now have in your hands an extremely valuable book. It is one of a series specially devised to aid the busy professional dealer in his everyday trading. It will also prove to be of great value to all collectors and those with goods to sell, for it is crammed with illustrations, brief descriptions and valuations of hundreds of antiques.

Every effort has been made to ensure that each specialised volume contains the widest possible variety of goods in its particular category though the greatest emphasis is placed on the middle bracket of trade goods rather than on those once - in - a - lifetime museum pieces whose values are of academic rather than practical interest to the vast majority of dealers and collectors.

This policy has been followed as a direct consequence of requests from dealers who sensibly realise that, no matter how comprehensive their knowledge, there is always a need for reliable, up-to-date reference works for identification and valuation purposes.

When using your Antiques and their Values to assess the worth of goods, please bear in mind that it would be impossible to place upon any item a precise value which would hold good under all circumstances. No antique has an exactly calculable value; its price is always the result of a compromise reached between buyer and seller, and questions of condition, local demand and the business acumen of the parties involved in a sale are all factors which affect the assessment of an object's 'worth' in terms of hard cash.

In the final analysis, however, such factors cancel out when large numbers of sales are taken into account by an experienced valuer, and it is possible to arrive at a surprisingly accurate assessment of current values of antiques; an assessment which may be taken confidently to be a fair indication of the worth of an object and which provides a reliable basis for negotiation.

Throughout this book, objects are grouped under category headings and, to expedite reference, they progress in price order within their own categories. Where the description states 'one of a pair' the value given is that for the pair sold as such.

Printed by Apollo Press, Dominion Way, Worthing, Sussex, England.
Bound by Newdigate Press, Vincent Lane, Dorking, Surrey, England.

# CONTENTS

Architects' Tables . . . . . . . . . . . .8
Breakfast/Supper Tables . . . . . . . .9
Card & Tea Tables . . . . . . . . . . . .10
   Central Column, Cabriole Leg . .10
   Central Column, Platform Base .11
   Central Column, Splay Feet. . . .12
   'D' End . . . . . . . . . . . . . . . .13
   Envelope . . . . . . . . . . . . . . . .14
   Half Round . . . . . . . . . . . . . .15
   Multiple Column . . . . . . . . . . .16
   Multiple Leg. . . . . . . . . . . . . .17
   Protruding Corners . . . . . . . . .18
   Rectangular Top . . . . . . . . . . .19
   Serpentine Front. . . . . . . . . . .20
   Shaped Top . . . . . . . . . . . . . .21
Carlton House Tables . . . . . . . . . .22
Centre Tables . . . . . . . . . . . . . . . .23
   Central Column. . . . . . . . . . . .25
   Stretcher Base. . . . . . . . . . . . .27
   Trestle Base . . . . . . . . . . . . . .29
Chess Top Tables. . . . . . . . . . . . . .31
Consol Tables . . . . . . . . . . . . . . . .33
Corner Tables . . . . . . . . . . . . . . . .36
Credence Tables . . . . . . . . . . . . . .36
Cricket Tables. . . . . . . . . . . . . . . .37
Dining Tables . . . . . . . . . . . . . . . .38
   Central Column, Cabriole Leg .41
   Central Column, Platform Base .42
   Central Column, Splay Feet,
   Round Top . . . . . . . . . . . . . .44
   Central Column, Splay Feet,
   Rectangular Top . . . . . . . . . .46
   Two Pillar . . . . . . . . . . . . . . .47
   Three Pillar . . . . . . . . . . . . . .48
Display Tables . . . . . . . . . . . . . . .49
Draw-Leaf Tables . . . . . . . . . . . . .50
Dressing Tables . . . . . . . . . . . . . .51
Drop-Leaf Tables. . . . . . . . . . . . . .52
Drum Tables. . . . . . . . . . . . . . . . .54
Games Tables . . . . . . . . . . . . . . .56
Gateleg Tables . . . . . . . . . . . . . . .58

Hall Tables. . . . . . . . . . . . . . . . . .62
Miscellaneous Tables . . . . . . . . . .63
Nests of Tables . . . . . . . . . . . . . . .64
Occasional Tables . . . . . . . . . . . . .65
   Gallery Top . . . . . . . . . . . . . .66
   Octagonal Top . . . . . . . . . . . .67
   Platform Base, Rectangular Top .68
   Platform Base, Round Top . . . .69
   Shelf Base . . . . . . . . . . . . . . .70
   Stretcher Base. . . . . . . . . . . . .72
   Three Legs . . . . . . . . . . . . . . .73
   Tripod Base, Rectangular Top . .74
   Tripod Base, Round Top. . . . . .75
   Tripod Base, Shaped Top . . . . .76
Pembroke Tables. . . . . . . . . . . . . .78
   'D' End Flaps . . . . . . . . . . . . .78
   Half Round Flaps . . . . . . . . . .80
   Rectangular Flaps . . . . . . . . . .82
   Shaped Flaps . . . . . . . . . . . . .83
Reading Tables . . . . . . . . . . . . . . .84
Refectory Tables . . . . . . . . . . . . . .85
Side Tables. . . . . . . . . . . . . . . . . .89
   Platform Base . . . . . . . . . . . .94
   Six Legs. . . . . . . . . . . . . . . . .95
   Stretcher Base. . . . . . . . . . . . .96
Sofa Tables . . . . . . . . . . . . . . . . .99
   Central Column. . . . . . . . . . . .100
   High Stretcher . . . . . . . . . . . .101
   Low Stretcher. . . . . . . . . . . . .102
   Multiple Column . . . . . . . . . . .104
Stands. . . . . . . . . . . . . . . . . . . . .105
Sutherland Tables . . . . . . . . . . . . .106
Triangular Top Tables . . . . . . . . . .108
Wakes Tables . . . . . . . . . . . . . . . .108
Work/Sewing Tables. . . . . . . . . . .109
   Central Column. . . . . . . . . . . .111
   Stretcher Base. . . . . . . . . . . . .114
Writing Tables . . . . . . . . . . . . . . .117
   Bureau Plat . . . . . . . . . . . . . .121
   Stretcher Base . . . . . . . . . . . .122
   Trestle Base . . . . . . . . . . . . . .123

# ARCHITECTS' TABLES

Chippendale architect's table of fine original colour, circa 1760. $625 £320

18th century mahogany architect's table with adjustable top and turned legs. $625 £320

Late 18th century mahogany architect's table. $880 £450

Late 18th century mahogany architect's table on a tripod base with brass castors. $1,270 £650

George II mahogany architect's table, 2ft.11½in. wide, circa 1760. $1,310 £680

A Late 18th century mahogany architect's table with rising top. $1,415 £725

Late 18th century mahogany architect's table, with ormolu handle. $1,515 £780

Chippendale period mahogany architect's table. $2,230 £1,240

A 19th century rosewood artist's table on a central column with splayed feet. $2,925 £1,500

An early Victorian mahogany supper table on a centre column with a shaped platform base and bun feet.
$245  £125

Early 19th century mahogany breakfast table on quadruple sabre leg base.
$340  £175

Mahogany supper table with crossbanded top, circa 1820.
$605  £310

George III mahogany supper table, circa 1810.
$700  £360

Regency mahogany breakfast table with a detachable leaf.
$740  £370

Chippendale period mahogany breakfast table.
$740  £370

Georgian mahogany breakfast table with tilt top on pillar and claws, with brass cup castors, 4ft.6in. x 3ft.9in. $860  £440

Unusual mid 18th century breakfast table in dark mahogany.
$1,120  £575

George III mahogany supper table, 39¾in. wide.
$1,440  £800

9

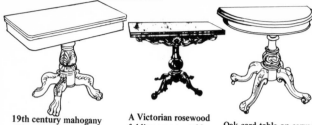

19th century mahogany oblong folding over tea table on carved and fluted pillar and four feet with paw toes, 3ft. wide.
$290 £150

A Victorian rosewood folding over tea table on pillar and carved claw base, 3ft. wide.
$310 £155

Oak card table on carved cabriole stand, about 1860, 74cm. high x 87cm. wide.
$340 £175

English mahogany card table with semi-circular swivelling top, circa 1845.
$390 £200

Victorian burr walnut folding top card table on cabriole legs.
$430 £220

Victorian walnut serpentine shaped, folding over card table, on carved central pillar and tripod feet, 3ft. diameter.
$460 £235

Rosewood fold over top stalk table on tripod supports.   $510 £270

Victorian burr walnut card table.
$575 £300

Victorian burr walnut fold over tea table.
$665 £340

## CENTRAL COLUMN, PLATFORM BASE     CARD AND TEA TABLES

Victorian pollard oak fold over card table, 3ft. wide.
$245 £125

A Victorian mahogany tea or games table, with swivelling top raised on a bulbous pillar and concave sided base.
$265 £135

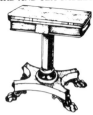

Rosewood card table, 3ft. wide, circa 1840.
$325 £180

Mahogany card table, probably Italian, circa 1830, 3ft. wide.
$370 £200

Victorian folding top rosewood card table on a central column with platform base.
$430 £220

Early Victorian rosewood card table on paw feet, 36in. wide.
$450 £230

Early 19th century burr walnut and ebony inlaid oblong folding over tea table, on carved pillar and block with ball feet, 3ft. wide. $470 £240

Late Regency brass inlaid rosewood folding top card table on a shaped platform with scroll brass inlaid feet.
$780 £400

Late 18th century yew wood and marquetry folding top games table.
$1,405 £720

11

## CARD AND TEA TABLES
## CENTRAL COLUMN, SPLAY FEET

**Early Victorian bird's eye maple tea table.**
$470  £240

**Early 19th century rosewood card table on splayed feet with brass claw castors.**
$585  £300

**William IV Gothic revival card table, 3ft.1in. wide, circa 1830.**
$585  £300

**Regency mahogany card table, circa 1815, 3ft. wide.**
$720  £400

**Regency rosewood fold over top card table, with satinwood bandings, 36in. wide.**
$1,025  £525

**George IV rosewood card table, 3ft. wide.**
$1,170  £600

**A Regency brass inlaid rosewood card table on a scroll base.**
$1,460  £750

**George IV brass inlaid rosewood card table, 3ft. wide.** $1,460  £750

**A Regency rosewood tea table on four concave shaped legs, 2ft. 11½in. wide.**
$1,560  £800

12

Late 19th century
ebonised card table
with bird's eye
maple panel.
$165 £85

Victorian mahogany
fold over tea table
with boxwood string
inlay, on turned legs.
$175 £90

George III tea table
in mahogany, on
turned legs.
$290 £150

Sheraton inlaid card
table on square
tapered legs, 3ft.
wide. $575 £295

Regency tea table
with a crossbanded
top and shaped legs.
$585 £300

Late 18th century
faded mahogany
card table with
satinwood crossband-
ing and ebony string
inlay. $780 £400

Dutch floral mar-
quetry fold over
card table.
$1,105 £600

A Regency period
fold over card table
in mahogany on lyre
supports with splay
feet.
$1,365 £700

Sheraton satinwood
inlaid card table on
tapered legs.
$1,680 £850

13

## CARD AND TEA TABLES
### ENVELOPE

Edwardian mahogany envelope card table. $165 £85

Edwardian mahogany envelope card table on shaped legs. $195 £100

Edwardian mahogany envelope card table with under-shelf. $195 £100

Edwardian mahogany envelope card table on cabriole legs. $195 £100

Edwardian mahogany card table with box-wood string inlay and tapered legs. $290 £150

Edwardian Sheraton revival mahogany envelope top folding card table. $290 £150

Edwardian inlaid mahogany envelope table on square tapering legs with cross stretchers. $340 £175

Victorian rosewood inlaid envelope card table with drawer and undershelf. $340 £175

French style rosewood and marquetry inlaid, serpentine shaped, envelope flap-over card table. $680 £350

14

19th century half
circular mahogany
folding card table
on cabriole legs.
$270 £135

Late 18th century
demi-lune card
table.
$625 £320

Georgian mahogany
fold over card table.
$755 £420

George II semi-
circular mahogany
card table, 1ft.8in.
wide, circa 1740.
$865 £480

A Sheraton period
half round, satin-
wood card table,
36in. wide.
$975 £500

18th century Dutch
walnut and marquetry
half-moon card table,
2ft.7in. high.
$1,015 £520

George III satinwood
card table, 40in. wide.
$2,315 £1,200

Queen Anne period
figured walnut fold-
ing top card table.
$2,440 £1,250

Adam period satin-
wood demi-lune
card table.
$3,900 £2,000

15

# CARD AND TEA TABLES
## MULTIPLE COLUMN

Victorian ebonised rectangular fold over card table, with burred maple inlay supported on four central turned and gilded pillars with key pattern feet.          $290  £150

Victorian inlaid walnut half round folding card table, 3ft. wide.          $360  £180

A Victorian walnut inlaid half circle folding over card table supported on four centre pillars and carved feet, 3ft. diam.          $390  £200

19th century mahogany folding over tea table, on four centre pillars and feet, 3ft. 4in. wide.          $390  £200

Victorian burr walnut and marquetry inlaid card table, 36in. wide.          $390  £200

19th century mahogany fold over top card table.          $635  £325

Mahogany card table on platform base, 29in. high, circa 1810.          $730  £375

Regency period satinwood card table, circa 1815.          $975  £500

Regency calamanderwood card table, 36in. wide.  $1,755  £900

16

Biedermeier cherry-wood extending folding top table, circa 1840.
$915  £500

Walnut games table with a hinged rectangular top and elaborately turned legs, 2ft.5½in. wide.
$1,070  £550

Antique mahogany games table with shaped triple fold top, 2ft.9in. wide.
$1,460  £750

William and Mary walnut card table with folding top and drawer.
$2,435  £1,250

A satinwood card table, circa 1785.
$2,435  £1,250

Rare George II mahogany triple top games table, 2ft.9in. wide.
$2,375  £1,250

A William and Mary marquetry card table, with three drawers to the frieze, 32in. wide.
$2,925  £1,500

Rare late 17th century walnut games table with fold over top, 33in. long.
$3,240  £1,800

Early 18th century George II mahogany triple top games table, 33¼in. wide.
$3,520  £1,825

17

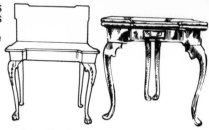

Late 19th century Queen Anne design mahogany oblong shaped folding card table, 84cm. wide. $390 £200

George II mahogany tea table with ball and claw front legs, 31in. wide. $830 £425

Georgian mahogany card table, on cabriole legs, 2ft.4in. wide. $890 £480

George II mahogany games table banded in kingwood. $975 £500

George I carved walnut games table crossbanded and feather strung, 86cm. wide. $1,755 £900

George I walnut card table, 2ft.11in. wide, circa 1720. $2,250 £1,250

Queen Anne marquetry folding top card table on fine cabriole legs. $2,925 £1,500

18th century laburnum wood card table with concertina action. $3,120 £1,600

Mid Georgian mahogany card table, 39¾in. wide. $4,860 £2,700

Late 19th century oak oblong fold over card table on turned legs with stretcher, 3ft. wide. $115 £60

Bamboo card table with fold over lacquered top, circa 1905. $175 £90

19th century mahogany folding top card table with beaded decoration. $230 £125

Painted satinwood card table, 1890's. $580 £300

19th century Dutch marquetry card table, 2ft.8in. high. $680 £350

Italian mahogany and tulipwood card table, 3ft.2½in. wide. $975 £500

18th century concertina action tea table in mahogany with finely carved cabriole legs with ball and claw feet. $1,200 £600

Early George III mahogany card table, 38in. wide. $2,030 £1,050

A very fine walnut card table by Thomas Johnson, 91.5cm. wide. $29,250 £15,000

## CARD AND TEA TABLES
## SERPENTINE FRONT

Victorian carved
walnut fold over
card table.
$275  £140

Mahogany tea table
of serpentine shape
with boxwood string-
ing, circa 1830.
$390  £200

Early 20th century
rosewood card table,
33in. wide.
$505  £280

Late 18th century Adam
style serpentine shaped
fold over card table on
tapered legs with block
toes.    $635  £325

Victorian burr
walnut card table.
$625  £340

Late 18th century
Dutch marquetry
inlaid card table.
$830  £425

19th century red boulle
card table mounted
with face mask ormolu
mounts, 95cm. wide.
$1,170  £600

Hepplewhite mahogany
card table, 3ft. wide, on
French cabriole legs.
$2,500  £1,350

Louis Phillipe tulip-
wood and marquetry
card table, 36in. wide.
$2,520  £1,400

A card table, probably by Crace, circa 1850, 39in. wide.
$235 £120

Victorian inlaid burr walnut folding top card table on a stretcher base. $260 £130

Victorian inlaid burr walnut card table. $460 £235

Burr walnut card table, circa 1870, 36in. wide.
$615 £330

19th century red boulle fold over swivel top card table. $680 £350

Fine Sheraton mahogany and branch satinwood card table, 35½in. wide, circa 1850.
$2,850 £1,500

Mid 19th century kingwood and tulipwood card table with ormolu decoration, 2ft.9in. wide.
$3,410 £1,750

Fine Queen Anne burr walnut card table, circa 1710, 2ft.10in. wide.
$5,490 £3,000

18th century inlaid walnut card table with circular recesses for gaming counters. $7,605 £3,900

21

## CARLTON HOUSE TABLES

Edwardian Carlton House writing table by Maple & Co.        $830  £425

Victorian mahogany Carlton House writing desk, banded with beechwood and ebony, 3ft.7in. wide.
$975  £500

Edwardian mahogany Carlton House writing desk. $975  £500

Edwardian Carlton House desk with in-set leather top, 48in. wide. $1,950  £1,000

Carlton House writing desk in painted satin-wood, 53½in. wide.
$2,445  £1,300

Regency mahogany Carlton House desk, 53¼in. wide.
$2,880  £1,600

Fine satinwood and marquetry Carlton House desk, 54in. wide. $3,110  £1,700

A fine Edwardian satin-wood Carlton House desk, on tapered legs.
$5,850  £3,000

Mahogany Carlton House writing table, circa 1797, 55½in. wide. $14,760  £8,200

Late 19th century
circular mahogany
centre table on cab-
riole legs with hoof
feet, 3ft.3in. diam.
$195  £100

An Edwardian inlaid
mahogany centre table
of two open and two
dummy drawers on
square tapering legs
with spade feet.
$485  £250

Scandinavian inlaid
low table, 1920's,
91.5cm. diameter.
$480  £260

19th century maho-
gany oblong table
with two pull-out
slides, carved apron
and cabriole legs, 3ft.
wide.  $585  £300

Rare solid walnut
centre table, circa
1740, 2ft.9in. wide,
possibly Portuguese.
$610  £340

Late 19th century
French oak and wal-
nut centre table with
ormolu embellish-
ments, 53in. wide.
$780  £400

Victorian burr wal-
nut centre table.
$760  £400

Unusual George III
mahogany centre
table, 2ft.7in. wide.
$810  £420

18th century Orien-
tal padouk centre
table, 52½ x 23in.
$975  £500

23

# CENTRE TABLES

Late 19th century centre table in rosewood, 28½in. high. $980 £510

18th century French marquetry centre table with ormolu mounts, 27in. wide. $1,170 £600

Late 19th century satinwood and marquetry centre table, 23in. wide. $1,190 £650

19th century marquetry centre table by L. W. Collman, 1850-1870. $1,460 £750

Mid 19th century red boulle serpentine table with good quality ormolu mounts, 148cm. wide. $1,850 £950

George II gilt centre table on cabriole legs, with a marble top. $1,950 £1,000

A Chinese padouk wood table profusely inlaid with mother-of-pearl. $3,315 £1,700

18th century Italian walnut centre table inlaid with tulipwood, 2ft.8in. square. $4,875 £2,500

George I gilt wood table. $5,310 £2,950

Late Victorian ebonised table with boxwood inlay. $255 £130

Early Victorian mahogany centre table on a shaped platform base with claw feet. $310 £160

Small Victorian mahogany centre table on a platform with claw feet. $310 £160

19th century walnut pedestal table with marquetry motifs, 35in. long. $430 £220

Small black and gilt centre table on a tripod base with figures inset in columns. $470 £240

Attractive rosewood two-drawer centre table, circa 1820, 27in. wide. $635 £325

Rosewood round table with string inlay and ormolu beaded edge, circa 1840, 50½in. diam. $830 £425

Early Victorian Continental salon table, 39in. diameter, with marble top. $875 £450

Mid 19th century Batavian ebony centre table, 47in. diameter. $1,060 £550

25

**Late George III satinwood centre table, 38¾in. diam.**
$1,100  £600

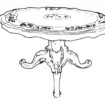

**Walnut Victorian centre table, 4ft. 3in. diameter.**
$1,755  £900

**Regency rosewood circular table with brass inlay and mountings, 46in. diameter.**
$1,950  £1,000

**Regency rosewood circular table with brass string inlay and a scroll base.**
$1,950  £1,000

**A brass inlaid rosewood centre table on a platform base with scroll feet.**
$1,950  £1,000

**Chinese marquetry and ivory inlaid rosewood table.**
$2,610  £1,450

**George IV oak and pollard oak centre table, 48½in. diam.**
$3,420  £1,900

**Walnut centre table, dated 1860, 53½in. diameter.**
$5,655  £2,900

**19th century Sevres porcelain and ormolu mounted centre table.** $6,825  £3,500

26

Bamboo tea table with lacquered top, circa 1900.
$75 £40

Edwardian shaped top mahogany centre table, on carved cabriole legs, 2ft.6in. diam. $85 £45

19th century hardwood table inlaid with mother-of-pearl, 3ft.
$490 £250

Late Gothic revival ebonised mahogany centre table, 1890's.
$745 £400

Oval centre table on tapering legs, 115 x 66cm. $755 £420

17th century Italian walnut, marquetry and ivory inlaid table, 48in. wide.
$790 £440

Late 18th century gilt wood centre table with marble top on tapering legs, 52cm. diameter.
$875 £450

A marquetry centre table on barley twist legs with cross stretchers. $1,170 £600

Jacobean walnut oblong table, of five spirally moulded legs with cross stretchers, 3ft.6in. long.
$1,265 £650

17th century Spanish
walnut centre table.
$1,460 £750

Rare German pine
pay table, with two
drawers, access to
top one by means of
sliding top.
$1,560 £800

19th century red
boulle centre table
with ormolu deco-
ration.
$1,950 £1,000

Fine 19th century
Dutch marquetry
centre table.
$2,340 £1,200

Rosewood coffee table
by Jacques Rhulmann,
circa 1925, 26½in. diam.
$2,860 £1,535

17th century Italian
walnut centre table,
55in. wide.
$3,780 £2,100

19th century Italian
carved gilt wood table
with inlaid marble top.
$4,875 £2,500

Louis XVI style mar-
quetry centre table in-
set with fine china
plaques and decorated
with ormolu.
$4,875 £2,500

Late 17th century Flemish
table, the legs formed as
classically draped men and
women, 3ft.5in. long.
$12,675 £6,500

Late 19th century
Victorian beech-
wood stretcher
table with ebony
string inlay.
$85  £45

Late 19th century
satin birch table.
$85  £45

Victorian walnut
stretcher table,
2ft.10in. long.
$115  £60

19th century maho-
gany stretcher table,
4ft.6in. long.
$155  £80

Victorian walnut table,
the centre with mar-
quetry panel, on turned
end supports, 2ft.10in.
wide.         $175  £90

17th century labur-
num wood Carolean
centre table.
$235  £120

Early 19th century
rosewood stretcher
table.  $245  £125

18th century walnut
chateau wine tasting
table with folding
top.    $275  £140

A fine quality light
oak centre table,
48in. wide, 1850's.
$275  £140

## CENTRE TABLES
## TRESTLE BASE

Victorian rosewood oblong table with drawer, 4ft.9in. long. $275 £140

Austrian centre table of ash with oval ends, 5ft.3in. wide, circa 1840. $310 £160

Finely figured Victorian rosewood table, 4ft.11in. wide, circa 1860. $515 £285

19th century carved rosewood centre table. $895 £460

Victorian walnut inlaid table with floral marquetry border and centre, 4ft.6in. wide. $895 £460

A fine mahogany table, the top cross-banded with acacia and inlaid with brass, circa 1840. $1,460 £750

16th century style Italian walnut trestle table, 19th century, 4ft.5in. long. $1,800 £1,000

Regency rosewood centre table, with inlaid cut brass, 36 x 20½in. $2,340 £1,200

Early 17th century Italian walnut centre table, 65in. wide. $3,590 £1,850

19th century walnut chess table on a platform base with bun feet. $125 £65

Victorian walnut, marquetry and parquetry inlaid circular games table, 1ft.8½in. diam. $150 £75

Victorian oval chess table in walnut on a stretcher base. $225 £115

Victorian papier mache table with inlaid mother-of-pearl chess board, 68cm. high. $235 £120

19th century French boulle chess table with engraved cut pewter inlays, 23in. wide. $275 £140

Victorian walnut Pembroke table, top inlaid with chess board, 67cm. $310 £160

Games and work table with inlaid top and interesting slide-out well. $350 £180

Early 19th century combined games and sewing table in rosewood.$605 £310

Regency mahogany games table complete with playing pieces.$800 £410

31

# CHESS TOP TABLES

Unusual walnut armorial chess table, 1850's.
$810 £420

A fine 19th century Tunbridge ware work table with drop flaps.
$875 £450

A good quality Welsh slate games table decorated with hunting scenes. $875 £450

19th century French walnut and marquetry table with a chess board top and ormolu mounts, 36in. wide.
$975 £500

Regency rosewood and parcel gilt games table, 59in. wide open.
$1,980 £1,100

George II mahogany games table.
$2,430 £1,350

18th century sofa games table with backgammon board, 2ft.6in. high, 2ft. 4½in. wide.
$3,120 £1,600

Late 18th century mahogany games and writing table, 109cm. wide.
$3,510 £1,800

Rare Regency mahogany games table, circa 1820, top, 3ft.5in. x 1ft.4in. $3,660 £2,000

Victorian mahogany
consol table, with a
figured marble top
and cabriole leg
front support.
$50  £25

20th century gilt
wood consol table
with carved and
pierced apron and
bracket.  $95  £50

Victorian cast iron
consol table with
marble top.
$155  £80

Wood and perspex
consol table, 1930's,
91.25cm. high.
$325  £170

Painted satinwood
consol table, 3ft.
1in. wide, circa
1780. $305  £170

A carved pine con-
sol table, with a
marble top, 24in.
wide, 30in. high.
$340  £175

Regency rosewood
consol table with
marble top, 60in.
wide. $340  £175

Early 19th century maho-
gany consol table, with a
serpentine front and gilt
enrichments. $485  £250

An Italian painted
consol table, circa
1790. $485  £250

# CONSOL TABLES

19th century finely
carved consol table,
originally gilded.
$580  £290

Early 19th century
rosewood pier table
with gilt decoration.
$975  £500

George II painted
consol table, 3ft.
5½in. wide.
$975  £500

Early 18th century
George I gilt wood
consol table, 48in.
wide.
$1,320  £680

Carved consol table
with marble top,
one of a pair.
$1,225  £680

A mahogany consol
table with finely
detailed carving and
green marble top,
52in. wide.
$1,365  £700

Gilt wood consol
table, 74in. long,
sold with overman-
tel mirror.
$1,280  £700

Mid 18th century German
white painted and parcel
gilt consol table, 27½in.
wide.          $2,135  £1,100

18th century gilt
consol table with
a carved eagle sup-
port.$2,340  £1,200

Early 18th century German carved oak consol table.
$3,315  £1,700

One of a pair of Empire ormolu mounted bronze and mahogany consols, 1ft.6in. wide.
$3,315  £1,700

George II mahogany consol table, 60in. wide. $3,300  £1,710

One of a pair of mid 18th century North Italian blue-painted and parcel gilt consol tables, 4ft.7in. wide.$3,780  £2,100

George II walnut consol table, 77in. wide. $4,630  £2,400

Louis XVI ormolu mounted mahogany consol desserte, one of a pair.
$4,680  £2,400

Fine lacquered wood and chrome consol by Donald Desky, circa 1927, 72in. wide.
$4,620  £2,485

Boulle consol table carved with caryatids, shells and acanthus leaves.
$48,750  £25,000

French consol table by J. H. Reisener with purpleheart and kingwood veneers on oak and a marble top, circa 1781. $360,750  £185,000

## CORNER TABLES

A 19th century mahogany inlaid corner table with drawers, on sabre front legs.
$145 £75

Unusual Sheraton mahogany corner table with platform.
$875 £450

Late 18th century Cuban mahogany tambour corner cabinet with tripod support, 1ft.6in. wide.
$1,460 £750

## CREDENCE TABLES

Late 19th century Charles I style oak credence table, 2ft. 6½in. high.
$575 £320

James I oak credence table with fold over top, the carved frieze inscribed SHL 1624.
$975 £500

James I oak credence table, circa 1610.
$1,190 £660

Mid 17th century oak credence table with carved frieze.
$1,365 £700

Late 17th century oak credence table with trapezoid top, 41¼in. wide.
$1,350 £750

James I oak credence table with fold over top, English about 1620. $1,950 £1,000

18th century pine-wood cricket table with stretchers. $85 £45

18th century pine-wood cricket table with a triangular shelf, 18in. diam. top. $145 £75

Late 18th century oak cricket table, circa 1790, 27½in. high. $145 £75

18th century oak and elm cricket table. $155 £80

Oak cricket table with shaped frieze, and chamfered inside edges to legs, 27in. diam., 28¾in. high, circa 1770. $165 £85

18th century oak cricket table, 22in. diameter, 20in. high. $195 £100

18th century fruit-wood cricket table with undershelf. $215 £110

Late 18th century walnut cricket table. $430 £220

17th century walnut cricket table, 20½in. wide. $585 £300

## DINING TABLES

Victorian mahogany telescopic dining table with a loose centre leaf. $145 £75

Victorian oval mahogany dining table with gadrooned edging and cabriole legs with claw feet.    $290 £150

A rosewood, rectangular, dining table, having 'U' shaped supports and glass protector, 6ft.6in. wide, 3ft.5in. broad.    $290 £150

Late 19th century mahogany oval telescopic dining table on turned legs, full extent 15ft.6in.    $320 £160

Oak dining table by J. J. Joass, 66in. long, circa 1940.    $355 £190

Oak telescopic dining table on six carved bulbous legs, (two folded up), 14ft.6in.    $390 £200

Victorian mahogany dining table in two parts on turned legs, 172cm. long.    $390 £200

Mahogany two flap dining table on six square tapered legs, circa 1820.    $485 £250

38

Late 19th century mahogany oval telescopic table with five loose leaves, full extent 11ft. $550 £275

Large mahogany boardroom table with a horse shoe pattern end, 21ft.6in. long. $780 £400

An early 19th century mahogany dining table, 7ft.7in. long fully extended. $800 £400

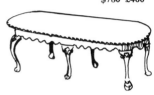

Early 20th century large mahogany dining table, 121in. long. $1,080 £560

A fine semi-circular, Irish drinking table, with additional flap. $1,170 £600

Fine mahogany dining table with lattice underframing, George IV, circa 1825, 7ft.6in. x 4ft.5in. $1,220 £625

18th century D-ended mahogany dining table. $1,260 £700

English walnut dining table, 60½in. diameter, circa 1935. $1,415 £760

39

## DINING TABLES

19th century oak dining table with carved frieze. **$1,500 £770**

An extremely large early 19th century mahogany extending table with a gate-leg centre section. **$1,950 £1,000**

George III D-end mahogany dining table, 9ft.9in. long extended. **$1,800 £1,000**

George III Honduras mahogany dining room table extending to 10ft.3in. x 4ft.2in. **$2,145 £1,100**

Regency mahogany extending dining table. **$2,145 £1,100**

An extremely large Georgian D-end dining table extending to 25ft. **$5,850 £3,000**

An unusual American mahogany extending dining table in the style of Duncan Phyle. **$6,825 £3,500**

Superb four pedestal mahogany dining table, overall length 3m.58cm. **$13,650 £7,000**

A Victorian burr
walnut and ebon-
ised loo table.
$290 £150

Victorian mahogany
four pillar pedestal
table, 114cm. wide.
$380 £195

A Victorian circular
mahogany dining
table on a tripod
base. $390 £200

Victorian mahogany
oval breakfast table
on a quadruple base
with centre pillar,
148cm. wide.
$390 £200

Victorian burr wal-
nut loo table on
quadruple base.
$585 £300

Victorian burr walnut
breakfast table with
boxwood string inlay
and an unusual base.
$780 £400

Victorian circular
walnut table, 52in.
diameter.
$1,130 £580

Victorian figured wal-
nut breakfast table
with marquetry inlaid
circular tilt top.
$1,460 £750

Continental marquetry
circular breakfast
table inlaid with a
medallion.
$2,925 £1,500

41

# DINING TABLES
## CENTRAL COLUMN, PLATFORM BASE

Late 19th century mahogany dining table on a pedestal base with claw feet.
$290 £150

Victorian snap top dining table quarter veneered in mahogany on a platform base with scroll feet.
$420 £210

Victorian carved oak table with a gadrooned edge and ornately carved base.
$535 £275

Early Victorian figured mahogany breakfast table, 121cm. diam.
$680 £340

Plum pudding mahogany pedestal dining table, circa 1840, 48in. diameter.
$680 £340

Early 19th century rosewood dining table with gilt paw feet.   $875 £450

George IV circular mahogany breakfast table, 3ft.5in. diam.
$875 £450

A fine rosewood dining table with a well figured oval top, on centre column with base standing on claw feet, circa 1850.   $1,070 £550

Early 19th century Dutch mahogany and floral marquetry table with oval top, 46¾in. wide.   $1,315 £675

Regency brass inlaid
rosewood table,
49½in. diameter.
$1,365  £700

Early 19th century
figured maple wood
round table, 52in.
diameter.
$1,460  £750

Regency breakfast
table in well figured
mellow rosewood
with brass inlay, 60in.
long, 38in. wide.
$1,560  £800

Victorian circular
inlaid rosewood
dining table with
scroll feet.
$1,560  £800

Early 19th century rose-
wood breakfast table in-
laid with brass on a platform base with scroll
feet.  $1,650  £850

Fine Regency period
breakfast table in
burr maple inlaid
with rosewood.
$2,435  £1,250

William IV maho-
gany hunting table
with a revolving
centre section.
$6,825  £3,500

Rosewood dining or
loo table, circa 1830,
1.68m. diameter.
$8,235  £4,500

Mid 19th century
mahogany dining
table, 58½in. diam.
$12,600  £7,000

43

## DINING TABLES
### CENTRAL COLUMN, SPLAY FEET, ROUND TOP

Circular oak dining table with a tip up top, 3ft.8in. diam., circa 1830.
$340  £175

Victorian ebonised loo table with ormolu decoration.$485  £250

Early 19th century mahogany pillar dining table.
$635  £325

Circular Regency mahogany breakfast table with three moulded sabre legs, 3ft.10½in. diameter.  $680  £350

Early 19th century figured walnut tip top table, 48in. diam.  $780  £410

English William IV circular rosewood dining table.
$1,170  £600

George IV mahogany breakfast table, 4ft.5in. diam.
$1,265  £650

Early 19th century mahogany pedestal table, 50in. diam.
$1,265  £650

Regency rosewood and brass inlaid circular top breakfast table, 4ft. diam.
$1,225  £680

Circular well figured mahogany dining table with string wood crossbanding and a reeded edge, circa 1810.
$1,365  £700

Georgian oval mahogany breakfast table with rosewood crossbanding, 54in. x 41in.
$1,415  £725

Early 19th century figured mahogany breakfast table with yew wood crossbanding and reeded legs.
$1,460  £750

Mid 19th century satinwood oval table, 48in. $1,620  £900

William IV circular mahogany breakfast table, 5ft. diameter, circa 1830.
$1,710  £950

An early 19th century breakfast table, the top inlaid with a bat's wing paterna and chevron crossbanding.
$2,145  £1,100

Regency rosewood tilt top table inlaid with brass. $3,600  £2,000

Early 19th century circular mahogany table on quadruple splay feet with brass castors.
$3,900  £2,000

Fine quality Regency inlaid satinwood table, 49in. diameter.
$4,875  £2,500

45

19th century mahogany oblong breakfast table on reeded legs with paw feet, 4ft.1in. wide. $390 £200

Early 19th century mahogany breakfast table with boxwood string inlay. $440 £225

Regency mahogany dining table, with a crossbanded top. $730 £375

Regency mahogany tilt top table with ebony string inlay and a reeded edge, 58in. wide. $925 £475

Late George III mahogany breakfast table, circa 1810, 5ft. wide. $865 £480

Good Regency mahogany breakfast table, circa 1810, 4ft.8½in. long. $1,350 £750

18th century mahogany breakfast table on reeded legs, 4ft.6in. x 3ft.4in. $1,560 £780

Regency zebra wood breakfast table with mahogany crossbanding, 4ft.8in. x 3ft.6in. $3,120 £1,600

19th century mahogany dining table with three spare leaves. $7,800 £4,000

20th century reproduction mahogany
dining table on two pillars with claw
feet, 6ft.6in. long.        $390 £200

Solid mahogany dining table which
makes two breakfast tables, circa 1830.
                           $1,170 £600

Regency two pillar mahogany dining
table.                    $1,560 £800

Sheraton mahogany D-ended pedestal
dining table.             $1,440 £800

Regency period extending dining table
in mahogany with an unusual split
pedestal action.          $1,655 £850

Late George III figured mahogany twin
pedestal dining table, turned columns
and splayed supports.  $2,145 £1,100

Regency two pillar dining table with
extra leaf, 7ft.2in. long fully extended,
circa 1820.             $2,340 £1,200

Original George IV two pillar dining
table, circa 1820.      $3,120 £1,600

# DINING TABLES
## THREE PILLAR

An early 19th century mahogany three pillar dining table, 145in. x 54in.
$1,655  £850

George III three pedestal mahogany dining table 137cm. x 356cm.
$1,990  £1,020

George III mahogany three pedestal dining table, 51in. x 152in. extended.
$2,340  £1,200

George III three pedestal table in mahogany, 10ft.5in. long.  $2,730  £1,400

Early 19th century mahogany three pillar pedestal table with brass claw feet, and a satinwood crossbanded top, 11ft.4in. long.  $2,925  £1,500

A mahogany three pillar table in good original condition, 5ft. wide, 12ft.9in. long, circa 1830.  $3,120  £1,600

A superb quality Georgian three pillar mahogany dining table. $6,825  £3,500

Fine Regency three pedestal dining table, 59¼in. wide.  $8,100  £4,500

Ebonised oblong
display table on
cabriole legs.
$195 £100

19th century mar-
quetry bijouterie
table with glazed
top and sides, 62cm.
wide. $275 £140

Edwardian inlaid
mahogany kidney
shaped display
table. $280 £145

Napoleon III kingwood
display table with glazed
oval top, 2ft. ½in. wide.
$390 £200

An Edwardian maho-
gany showcase, in-
laid in various woods
and painted bell
flowers, 30in. x 20in.
$450 £230

19th century heart
shaped specimen
table in satinwood
with floral marquetry
decoration.$485 £250

Satinwood display
table, circa 1900,
24½in. wide.
$480 £250

A 19th century maho-
gany display table, on
cabriole legs, with
chased ormolu mounts
and feet, 27in. wide.
$700 £360

French Empire circu-
lar display table in
burr yew with fine
quality ormolu mounts.
$1,265 £650

49

# DRAW-LEAF TABLES

An Edwardian burr walnut veneered draw-leaf table on cabriole legs, 5ft.6in. wide.                    **$95  £50**

Early 20th century 'Elizabethan' oak draw-leaf table, 39in. wide.**$425  £220**

17th century Dutch draw-leaf dining table, 27in. x 51in., extending to 93in.
                    **$1,655  £850**

17th century Dutch oak draw-leaf table, 28in. wide.    **$2,185  £1,150**

Oak Dutch draw-leaf table.
                    **$3,410  £1,750**

17th century Flemish pale oak draw-leaf dining table, 90in. wide.
                    **$5,820  £3,000**

An Elizabethan oak draw-leaf table, 6ft. long when closed, 11ft.2in. long fully extended.        **$7,800  £4,000**

17th century Swiss walnut draw-leaf table on turned baluster legs.
                    **$8,640  £4,800**

Late 19th century king-wood poudreuse on tapering cabriole legs, 2ft.9in. wide.
$360  £200

19th century French inlaid rosewood boudoir table. $730  £375

Mid 19th century walnut and ormolu mounted toilet table, signed Tahn of Paris, 53cm. wide.  $780  £400

Georgian red walnut dressing table with rising top, 2ft.7in. wide.  $875  £450

Walnut toilet table, circa 1830, 2ft.11in. wide.  $830  £450

A Regency mahogany dressing table, 42in. wide.  $1,170  £600

Rare Sheraton period mahogany 'D' table, 36in.wide, circa 1780.
$1,265  £650

German ormolu mounted marquetry poudreuse, 2ft. 4in. wide, circa 1750.
$2,700  £1,500

Dressing table by Emile-Jacques Rhulmann, circa 1920, 43½in. wide.
$13,310  £6,655

# DROP-LEAF TABLES

Late 18th century oak drop-leaf cottage dining table, on square legs. $165 £85

Mahogany dining table on square tapering legs, full extent 5ft.3in. $175 £90

A Victorian ebonised drop-leaf table, the oval top with box-wood stringing and stylised paterae, 4ft. 3in. wide. $195 £100

George III mahogany table with two drop-leaves, full length 3ft. $240 £120

A 19th century mahogany inlaid half circle table, with a drop-leaf, on square taper-ing legs, 2ft.6in. diameter. $240 £120

Early 19th century Cuban mahogany drop-leaf table on pad feet. $230 £125

Late 18th century mahogany drop-leaf dining table with six legs. $480 £240

Late 18th century mahogany spider leg side table, 2ft. 6½in. x 13in. $480 £260

Late 18th century oak drop-leaf dining table opening to 5ft. long. $585 £300

Early George I mahogany pad foot dining table with two large flaps. $730 £375

George II mahogany drop-leaf table, 3ft. high, circa 1750. $700 £390

A large mahogany inlaid and crossbanded oval dining table with club feet, 5ft.1in. wide. $960 £480

A rare red walnut Queen Anne pad foot dining table, circa 1710. $1,200 £600

17th century oak well table on turned legs. $1,560 £800

Fine George I gateleg table in Virginia Red walnut, with well figured top, 57 x 48in., circa 1725. $1,560 £800

Queen Anne mahogany drop-leaf dining table, 48in. wide. $2,090 £1,100

Dutch marquetry gate leg dining table, 51in. wide. $3,105 £1,600

George III mahogany hunting table, 8ft.10in. long, circa 1780. $2,970 £1,650

## DRUM TABLES

Small Victorian mahogany drum table. $585 £300

Early Victorian mahogany drum table by Robert Strahan & Co., Dublin. $730 £400

Mahogany drum table, circa 1840, 3ft.10in. diam. $1,260 £650

George III mahogany drum table. $1,260 £700

Unusual George III mahogany drum top table, 3ft.7in. diam. $1,350 £750

A Regency burr elm drum table with good patina. $1,655 £850

George III revolving top table on a centre column with splayed feet. $1,655 £850

Regency mahogany circular library table, 3ft.4in. diam., circa 1820. $1,620 £900

William IV circular mahogany library table, 4ft.2in. diam., circa 1830. $1,710 £950

A fine quality Regency period rosewood library table.
$2,340 £1,200

George III inlaid mahogany drum top rent table, 96cm. diam.
$2,340 £1,200

A good quality Regency period mahogany drum table with ormolu enrichments.
$2,340 £1,200

19th century boulle circular drum table with heavy ormolu mounts.
$2,435 £1,250

Late 18th century library table in mahogany with ebony stringing on the legs and round the frieze.
$2,925 £1,500

George III mahogany drum table, 42¼in. diam. $3,605 £1,850

George II mahogany rent table with twelve drawers, 4ft. 6in. diam.
$4,385 £2,250

Rare George III mahogany library table, 5ft.3in. diam.$9,750 £5,000

Fine George III mahogany rent table, 42in. diam.
$9,000 £5,000

# GAMES TABLES

William IV rosewood games table, 1ft.8½in. wide. $380 £200

19th century Indian inlaid games table, 32¼in. wide. $380 £200

Compact rosewood games table, circa 1860. $440 £225

Egyptian parquetry games table. $485 £250

French circular marquetry games table with reversible top. $585 £300

An 18th century parquetry games table, on slender cabriole legs. $925 £475

Small Regency rosewood games table on quadruple sabre legs, 2ft.9in. high. $925 £475

A 19th century walnut games table, 3ft. wide. $1,070 £550

Regency mahogany games table with lifting top, 22in. wide. $1,080 £600

56

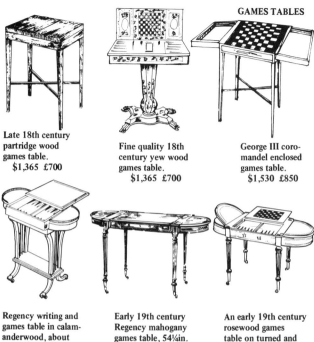

Late 18th century
partridge wood
games table.
$1,365 £700

Fine quality 18th
century yew wood
games table.
$1,365 £700

George III coro-
mandel enclosed
games table.
$1,530 £850

Regency writing and
games table in calam-
anderwood, about
1800. $3,120 £1,600

Early 19th century
Regency mahogany
games table, 54¼in.
wide. $3,960 £2,050

An early 19th century
rosewood games
table on turned and
reeded legs.
$8,285 £4,250

Superb 17th century
South German games
table complete with
games.$8,775 £4,500

A fine games table
in the manner of
E. Butler.
$10,725 £5,500

South German games
table decorated in
mother-of-pearl and
tortoiseshell, 41¼ x
29½in.$31,200 £16,000

# GATELEG TABLES

A Victorian oval oak gateleg table, with two leaves on turned legs, full width 3ft.2in.
$65 £35

Victorian oak gateleg table, with barley twist supports.
$95 £50

Victorian oak gateleg dining table with a carved border and spiral legs.
$155 £80

Oak gateleg table with drawer, circa 1740, 33 x 38in. when open.
$310 £160

18th century oak oval gateleg table with ground level stretchers, 80cm. wide. $330 £170

Small 18th century oak gateleg table, 28¼in. wide.
$340 £175

Early 18th century oak gateleg table, 43 x 53in. extended.
$485 £250

A fine walnut gateleg table, circa 1700, 45in. wide when open, 27in. high.
$585 £300

A well figured oak gateleg table, in original condition, 44in. wide, circa 1750. $680 £350

Early and unusual gateleg table in dark oak, 27in. high, circa 1730.    $780 £400

Late 17th century oak oval gateleg dining table, 4ft.8½in. opened.  $910 £455

A large 18th century elm gateleg table with drawer, 5ft.2in. wide.    $910 £455

17th century oak and fruitwood gateleg table, 35in. wide, open. $915 £500

Mid 17th century oak drop-leaf table. $975 £500

William and Mary oak gateleg table, 3ft.6in. long.    $970 £500

William and Mary oak gateleg table, circa 1690, 4ft.6in. open.    $935 £520

Unusual Charles II oak gateleg table, 3ft.1in. wide, circa 1680. $1,025 £550

Oak gateleg table, 52in. wide, circa 1700. $1,170 £600

59

# GATELEG TABLES

17th century oak
gateleg table with
Spanish feet, 54 x
51in.
$1,170 £600

17th century Spanish
walnut gateleg table
with oval top, 4ft.2in.
wide. $1,170 £600

Rare 17th century
oak gateleg table
with plain gate
supports, 27½in.
high. $1,170 £600

Louis XIV walnut
double gateleg table,
circa 1680, 4ft.11in.
open. $1,115 £620

Oak gateleg table
with oval top,
circa 1690, 4ft.8in.
long. $1,300 £700

Large mid 17th
century walnut
gateleg table, with
barley twist sup-
ports, 41in. wide.
$1,460 £750

Charles II small
oak gateleg table,
circa 1685, 2ft.8in.
wide. $1,350 £750

Late 17th century yew
wood gateleg oval
table, extending to
58in. $1,560 £800

Charles II oak gate-
leg table, circa 1680,
5ft. 11½in. wide
open. $1,465 £800

**Large early 18th century gateleg table. $1,560 £800**

**Charles I oak gateleg table, circa 1640, 5ft.6in. extended. $1,530 £850**

**William and Mary oak gateleg table, circa 1690, 59½in. diameter. $2,435 £1,250**

**Large Charles II oak gateleg table, circa 1680, 5ft.10in. open. $2,520 £1,400**

**William and Mary turned maple gateleg table, 48in. long. $3,315 £1,700**

**Charles II gateleg table, circa 1680, 2ft.4in. high. $3,660 £2,000**

**An extremely rare late 17th century oak gateleg table. $5,360 £2,750**

**Early English oak gateleg table with barley twist legs, circa 1780. $5,850 £3,000**

**18th century Cuban mahogany double gateleg table. $6,825 £3,500**

# HALL TABLES

A late Victorian hall table with two end drawers on square tapering legs, 3ft.1in. wide.    $65  £35

A carved oak hall table with drawer and panel back, 3ft 6in. wide.
$100  £50

Late 19th century carved oak oblong hall table of Italian design, 105cm.
$125  £65

19th century rosewood hall table with shaped marble top. $145  £75

A 19th century oak hall table with a drawer and concave shaped ends, 3ft.8in. wide.    $190  £95

A 19th century oak hall table with two drawers, on turned legs, 4ft. wide.
$190  £95

A 19th century oak hall table, with a thick slate top, on square panelled legs, 5ft. wide.
$245  £125

Small Regency hall table. $250  £140

An 18th century oak hall table with inlaid top and three drawers, with cabriole legs on brass club feet, 3ft.2in.
$830  £425

Victorian mahogany
bedside table.
$50 £25

18th century mahogany accounting table,
24in. wide, inlaid with
marquetry panels.
$585 £300

Rosewood marquetry
jardiniere, circa 1900,
possibly French.
$650 £360

A pseudo-Gothic
oak table.
$730 £375

Mahogany 'surprise'
table, which becomes
a drinking cabinet.
$1,010 £560

Chinese padouk
wood 'altar table',
of the 18th century,
5ft.7in. wide.
$1,365 £700

17th century oak
table settle of
good colour.
$1,460 £750

Louis XV marquetry
table d'accoucher,
2ft.2½in. wide.
$1,655 £850

17th century
German pay
table in oak
and pine.
$1,950 £1,000

63

# NESTS OF TABLES

A reproduction nest of three walnut tables with serpentine fronts, on cabriole legs.
$115 £60

A set of three Edwardian mahogany oval tables with satinwood banding on trestle bases.
$155 £80

19th century nest of four lacquered tables in good condition, circa 1840.
$330 £165

Quartetto of early 19th century black lacquered tea tables.
$390 £200

A nest of four mid 19th century papier mache tables, including a games table.
$730 £375

George III mahogany quartetto tables, 27in. high.
$730 £375

Set of early 19th century mahogany and rosewood banded quartetto tables, 53cm. wide. $1,460 £750

A fine set of 18th century rosewood quartetto tables with cock beaded tops and crossbanded edges.
$1,950 £1,000

Set of four marquetry tables with glass tops, circa 1900, by Galle.
$2,330 £1,200

Oriental carved black-wood and inlaid circular coffee table on a folding stand, 61cm. diameter. $50 £25

Indo-Portugese hardwood table inlaid with ivory and mother-of-pearl. $195 £100

Sheraton style satinwood occasional table. $350 £180

19th century French walnut and kingwood occasional table, 29 x 19in. $895 £460

George III small satinwood marquetry table, 1ft.5¾in. wide. $1,405 £780

Louis XV parquetry table, circa 1760, 2ft. wide. $1,840 £1,000

Late 17th century Spanish walnut table.$1,950 £1,000

Small George II marble topped red walnut table, 1ft.10in. wide. $3,780 £2,100

Late George III satinwood and marquetry table, 26in. wide. $7,560 £4,200

## OCCASIONAL TABLES
## GALLERY TOP

Late 18th century
mahogany tripod
table with bird
cage action.
$485  £250

Chippendale mahogany
serpentine shaped table
on fluted turned pillar,
2ft. wide x 1ft.6in.
$605  £310

A George II maho-
gany silver or china
table, circa 1740.
$975  £500

Regency mahogany
dumb waiter on
tripod stand.
$1,025  £525

Late George II maho-
gany tripod table, 2ft.
high.  $1,460  £750

Chippendale mahogany
silver table, circa 1763.
$2,415  £1,250

George II mahogany
tripod table, 2ft.6in.
high.  $2,535  £1,300

Mahogany urn table
with serpentine carved
gallery, on cabriole
legs, circa 1770.
$3,120  £1,600

Chippendale octagonal
top tripod kettle stand,
1ft.10in. high x 10in.
wide, table top.
$3,705  £1,900

Victorian octagonal ebonised and bird's eye maple pedestal table, 1ft.10in. wide. $40 £20

A mahogany octagonal table on pillar, 2ft.4in. high. $50 £25

English two-tier occasional table with Japanese lacquer panels, circa 1880-1905. $85 £45

Edwardian inlaid mahogany shaped top table, 2ft.4in. diam. $115 £60

19th century Japanese table with lacquered top. $115 £60

19th century marble octagonal top occasional table in mahogany, 12in. wide. $195 £100

Late 19th century walnut and marquetry tip top table. $500 £260

A rosewood rent collector's table with ten brass slots for coins, on mahogany pedestal and base. $525 £270

Octagonal shaped centre table, circa 1850, 42in. wide, probably by Crace. $830 £460

## OCCASIONAL TABLES
## PLATFORM BASE, RECTANGULAR TOP

Mahogany oblong table on octagonal pillar and block, 2ft.4in. wide.
$65  £35

Early Victorian mahogany snap top table on a turned column with a shaped platform base and paw feet. $75  £40

Victorian rosewood table with drawer, 18in. square.
$85  £45

Victorian oak table on centre column, with tripod base, 3ft.5in. x 2ft.11in.
$165  £85

William IV marble top table with brass edging.  $390  £200

An unusual small mid 19th century Gothic oak table with drawer.
$440  £225

Fine oak occasional table, circa 1830, 31in. wide.
$405  £225

Regency rosewood occasional table with brass feet.
$585  £300

William IV table, 2ft.3in. wide, circa 1830. $780  £400

68

Small Victorian rose-
wood occasional
table, 20in. diameter.
$40  £20

Circular rosewood
side table on a
fluted tripod and
shaped platform
base.  $145  £75

Victorian papier
mache tripod
table inlaid with
mother-of-pearl.
$155  £80

Early Victorian cast
iron pedestal table
painted with a view
of shipping in the
Clyde.  $340  £175

Victorian papier
mache occasional
table, 22in. high.
$400  £210

Regency carved
table with marble
top, 2ft.8in. diam.,
circa 1815.
$830  £425

Unusual William IV
tripod table, 2ft.9in.
diameter, circa 1835.
$1,260  £700

One of a pair of William
IV circular occasional
tables, 2ft. diameter.
$2,160  £1,200

French Empire guer-
idon with a porphyry
top, with mirror
panels, 76.2cm. diam.
$3,120  £1,600

69

## OCCASIONAL TABLES
## SHELF BASE

Small Edwardian table with a scratched carved top.
$30 £15

Edwardian mahogany occasional table with a braced undertier and shaped legs.
$95 £50

Victorian bamboo occasional table with lacquered top.
$95 £50

Edwardian oval mahogany and satinwood banded occasional table on shaped legs.
$105 £55

Victorian burr walnut salon occasional table.
$195 £100

Art furniture design two-tier table in ebony and specimen wood, circa 1880.
$280 £145

Early 20th century mahogany parquetry etagere, 30¼in. high.
$305 £170

Edwardian satinwood marquetry two-tier table with shaped gallery and urn finials, 2ft.4in. high.
$340 £175

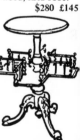

Victorian walnut dumb waiter on tripod cabriole legs, 18½in. wide. $350 £180

## SHELF BASE

## OCCASIONAL TABLES

French fruitwood and marquetry inlaid kidney shaped table, 19th century.
$440 £225

Regency period mahogany etagere with fine ormolu mounts.
$535 £275

Louis XV style kingwood and rosewood banded serpentine shaped table, 19th century. $535 £275

Yew wood hexagonal table with glass top, 29in. high, circa 1850. $555 £285

A Regency period green marble table with ormolu decoration. $780 £400

Louis Phillipe kingwood etagere decorated with Sevres plaques and ormolu mounts. $1,655 £850

Sheraton period tulipwood tricoteuse of French influence, 27in. x 16in.
$1,950 £1,000

Satinwood occasional table with rosewood inlay, circa 1790, 2ft. 4in. high x 1ft.9in. deep. $3,410 £1,750

Ormolu and porcelain mounted table a cafe by B.V.R.B., 26in. high.
$243,750 £125,000

## OCCASIONAL TABLES STRETCHER BASE

A 19th century mahogany table with spindle end supports and stretchers, 1ft.7in. wide.
$85 £45

Late 19th century Oriental rosewood occasional table.
$95 £50

Circular Victorian table in prime condition.
$165 £85

Late 19th century circular satinwood occasional table, 2ft. diameter.
$305 £170

Unusual Regency brass inlaid simulated rosewood mirror top table.
$400 £205

Louis XVI style, oval gilt wood table with inset marble top, 70cm.
$485 £250

William IV parquetry table on turned trestle supports, 2ft.2in. wide.
$720 £400

Amboyna wood table of Louis XVI design.
$1,265 £650

Sheraton satinwood occasional table, circa 1790.
$1,365 £700

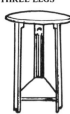

Edwardian oak occasional table. $30 £15

Victorian rosewood gypsy table with bobbin legs and a fringed top. $50 £25

19th century bird's eye maple two-tier effect table inlaid with mother-of-pearl. $145 £75

Victorian pub table with 21in. diam. copper top, circa 1860. $155 £80

Louis XVI style satinwood occasional table crossbanded with mahogany with an ormolu gallery and shaped supports. $390 £200

Restoration circular table, circa 1820, 2ft.8in. wide. $700 £380

Oak domino table by Charles Rennie Mackintosh, 79cm. high, circa 1911. $960 £520

A French marquetry drum shaped pedestal chest with ormolu mounts and galleries, 15in. diameter. $1,170 £600

Louis XV transitional circular ormolu mounted table a ouvrage stamped RVLC JME, 1ft.2½in. diam. $8,285 £4,250

73

## OCCASIONAL TABLES
### TRIPOD BASE, RECTANGULAR TOP

A 19th century Cairo mother-of-pearl inlaid oblong wine table on a central pillar with tripod base. $30 £15

19th century mahogany oblong table on pillar and claw base, 1ft.11in. wide. $80 £40

19th century lacquered oblong table on tree trunk stem. $85 £45

Victorian mahogany pedestal table with drawer on a centre column with shaped legs. $105 £55

19th century mahogany snap over table, inlaid with ebony, on turned central pillar with tripod feet. $175 £90

An Italian walnut table, the top parquetry and marquetry inlaid, on central pillar and tripod base, 2ft. 8in. wide. $215 £110

Chippendale period mahogany wine table with claw and ball feet, 27in. high, circa 1780. $280 £145

A 19th century oyster-shell walnut and rosewood banded table on a central pillar, 2ft.3in. wide. $290 £150

Regency rosewood tripod table, 15½in. square. $395 £220

19th century circular mahogany tripod table with a barley twist centre column. $65 £35

Victorian rosewood table with barley twist supports and tripod base with cabriole legs. $95 £50

George III mahogany snap top table. $120 £65

Victorian burr walnut table with boxwood string inlay and carved cabriole legs. $225 £115

Georgian mahogany tripod table, circa 1780. $255 £130

Unusual oak circular table with inlaid top, the central band carved 'Rowland Naylor, 1862', 22in. diam. $535 £275

George IV parquetry occasional table, circa 1825, 24½in. wide. $610 £340

18th century Dutch marquetry snap top table. $780 £400

A rare George II solid yew wood tripod table with brass wire inlay, 2ft.3¾in. diam. $1,460 £750

## OCCASIONAL TABLES
## TRIPOD BASE, SHAPED TOP

Small Victorian mahogany tripod table.  $50 £25

A reproduction circular table with pie crust border, on pillar and carved tripod feet, 19½in. diam. $95 £50

Victorian rosewood tray top table, 16in. $145 £75

Small 19th century walnut occasional table with clover leaf top.$175 £90

18th century mahogany shaped top table, 81cm. diam. $195 £100

19th century mahogany tripod table of Chippendale design with top and base support carved, 30in. high. $245 £125

Victorian shaped top table decorated with classical figures in penwork. $245 £125

Victorian papier mache table on a tripod platform base with scroll feet.  $275 £140

19th century lacquered snap top table.  $275 £140

## TRIPOD BASE, SHAPED TOP

## OCCASIONAL TABLES

Mid Victorian papier mache occasional table, top painted with a Highland scene, 1ft.9in. wide.
$280 £145

An Irish Chippendale style mahogany circular table with tip up action and tripod feet, 2ft.3in. diam.$440 £225

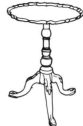

George II scallop and pie crust edge tripod table in finely figured mahogany.$440 £225

George III mahogany circular supper table, 29½in. diameter.
$485 £250

George III mahogany tripod table with tilting top, 31in. diameter. $925 £475

A George III pie crust table on claw and ball feet.$1,170 £600

A good George II mahogany supper table. $1,170 £600

George II mahogany tripod table, 2ft.6in. diameter.$1,225 £680

18th century Chippendale mahogany pedestal table with carved pillar and splayed tripod.
$1,950 £1,000

77

# PEMBROKE TABLES
## 'D' END FLAPS

Late Victorian stripped pine Pembroke table with drawer, on turned legs.
$55 £30

Edwardian reproduction walnut Pembroke table on cabriole legs with ball and claw feet, 2ft.3in. wide. $125 £65

Mahogany Pembroke table, with one drawer, circa 1830.
$265 £135

Late 18th century mahogany Pembroke table on square tapering legs with castors.
$285 £145

Sheraton period mahogany Pembroke table with crossbanded top and brass toe castors, 33in. wide. $340 £175

Early 18th century mahogany Pembroke table crossbanded with bird's eye maple, on square tapering legs, 2ft.9in. wide when open. $535 £275

Late 18th century mahogany Pembroke table with shell inlay.
$535 £275

Mahogany Pembroke table on reeded legs, circa 1800.
$620 £310

Georgian partridge wood Pembroke table on finely turned legs.
$840 £320

George III satinwood
and rosewood banded
Pembroke table.
$700  £360

Mahogany pedestal
Pembroke table,
42in. x 46in. x 29in.
high, circa 1800.
$830  £425

Small Sheraton period
drop-flap occasional
table.   $875  £450

Sheraton mahogany
and satinwood banded
Pembroke table, 30in.
wide.   $935  £520

Regency rosewood
Pembroke table,
44½in. wide, open.
$1,160  £600

Early 19th century
George III faded rose-
wood Pembroke table,
41¾in. wide.
$1,430  £740

Late 18th century
satinwood Pembroke
table inlaid with rib-
bons and swags.
$1,560  £800

George III satinwood
Pembroke table, circa
1780, 3ft.3in. wide,
open.  $2,125  £1,100

Regency mahogany
Pembroke writing table,
circa 1810, 3ft.4½in.
wide.  $2,125  £1,100

# PEMBROKE TABLES
## HALF ROUND FLAPS

Late 19th century mahogany oval Pembroke table on square tapered legs, 92cm. wide. $115 £60

19th century Sheraton style inlaid mahogany and satinwood banded oval Pembroke table, 76cm. wide. $290 £150

A neat satinwood oval occasional table with painted Adam designs. $330 £170

Late 18th century Adam design inlaid mahogany and kingwood banded Pembroke table. $390 £200

Small late 18th century oval Pembroke table in mahogany. $505 £280

Small late 18th century mahogany Pembroke table with drawer, on square tapering legs. $585 £300

Painted satinwood Pembroke table, circa 1890, 36in. wide, open. $660 £360

Fine George III mahogany inlaid oval Pembroke table in Adam style, 41in. wide. $780 £400

Sheraton period mahogany Pembroke table. $820 £420

80

An early 19th century
mahogany Pembroke
table on tapered legs
with spade feet.
$925  £475

An unusual George III
banded mahogany
Pembroke table.
$975  £500

Sheraton period satin-
wood and tulipwood
crossbanded Pembroke
table, 37in. wide.
$1,070  £550

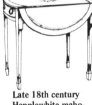

Late George III satin-
wood Pembroke table,
2ft.5in. open.
$1,365  £700

Late 18th century
Hepplewhite maho-
gany Pembroke table
with oval flaps, taper-
ing legs and spade
feet.  $1,560  £800

Late 18th century Dutch
marquetry circular drop-
leaf table, circa 1790,
4ft.10in. diam.
$2,160  £1,200

George III inlaid
satinwood Pembroke
table, 2ft.5in. x 1ft.
9in.  $2,730  £1,400

George III inlaid satin-
wood Pembroke table,
circa 1785.
$4,210  £2,300

A fine George III
satinwood Pembroke
table.$8,385  £4,300

# PEMBROKE TABLES
## RECTANGULAR FLAPS

20th century George III mahogany Pembroke table, 38½in. wide. $195 £100

Mahogany library table, signed 'Gillow', with drop leaves and gold tooled leather top, 30in. high. $525 £270

Georgian inlaid mahogany Pembroke table. $730 £375

Mahogany Pembroke table of medium colour with an elegant cross stretcher, 41in. wide when open, circa 1770. $975 £500

19th century burr walnut and cedarwood Pembroke table, 28½in. wide. $1,175 £610

Early George III laburnum wood veneered Pembroke table, 3ft.4in. wide. $1,115 £620

Small Sheraton period satinwood Pembroke table crossbanded in kingwood. $1,755 £900

Early George III Pembroke table, circa 1765, 1ft.8in. closed. $2,415 £1,250

Rare George III satinwood 'Harlequin' Pembroke table, 36¼in. wide, open. $7,200 £4,000

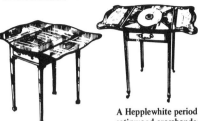

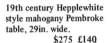

19th century Hepplewhite style mahogany Pembroke table, 29in. wide.
$275 £140

A Hepplewhite period satinwood crossbanded and boxwood inlaid Pembroke table, with serpentine shaped flaps, 3ft. wide. $485 £250

Late 19th century satinwood Pembroke table, 32½in. wide.
$700 £360

A fine Sheraton mahogany Pembroke table on square tapering legs, circa 1780. $840 £430

18th century Pembroke table in mahogany with rope decoration 2ft. 4½in. high, 3ft.2¾in. max. width.
$1,320 £660

Late 18th century satinwood Pembroke table with butterfly wing leaves.
$1,950 £1,000

Late George III satinwood and rosewood Pembroke table with two flap top, 40in. wide. $2,520 £1,400

An elegant George III mahogany Pembroke table in the French Hepplewhite style.
$4,095 £2,100

George III mahogany Pembroke table, 37½in. wide, open.
$9,900 £5,500

# READING TABLES

Victorian mahogany reading stand with a brass and iron base.
$70 £35

A rare Georgian mahogany draughtsman's table, the top adjustable to several positions, circa 1810. $640 £320

Georgian mahogany reading table.
$830 £460

Early 19th century mahogany reading stand with a platform base and lion's paw feet. $340 £175

18th century mahogany easel table on pad feet. $635 £325

A George III combined book trolley and reading stand in mahogany, 28½in. wide, circa 1810.
$975 £500

Rosewood reading table with drawer and candle slides, circa 1850.
$505 £260

Regency rosewood stand with reeded legs. $830 £425

George III mahogany reading table, 24in. wide.
$3,420 £1,900

84

Reproduction oak refectory table on bulbous end supports, 6ft. long.
$245 £125

'Mouseman' oak buffet table, 60in. long, 1936-40.
$295 £160

20th century oak dining table, 88in. long.
$500 £260

Farmhouse oak refectory table with honey-coloured patination, circa 1730, 56in. long x 26½in. wide x 29½in. high.
$680 £350

A fine 18th century elm refectory table, 7ft.6in. long.
$875 £450

Oak refectory table in original conditon, 7ft.1in. long, 29in. wide, circa 1750.
$875 £450

Late 19th century reproduction oak refectory table.
$905 £465

Oak refectory table with ground level stretchers, circa 1700.
$1,170 £600

# REFECTORY TABLES

A Dutch 18th century oak refectory table, with bevelled top, inlaid frieze and carved baluster legs, 6ft. x 2ft.9in. $1,170 £600

A rare cherrywood refectory table, 31½in. wide, 7½ft. long, 29½in. wide. $1,170 £600

An early oak refectory table with oblong top, on carved underframe, having turned legs and stretchers, 75in. x 31in. $1,265 £650

George II oak refectory table, 7ft.3in. long, circa 1760. $1,560 £800

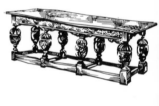

18th century elm tavern table with attractive patina. $1,610 £825

Large carved oak refectory table, 11ft. 6in. long. $1,620 £900

18th century pale oak centre table, 72in. wide. $1,755 £900

17th century oak and beechwood centre table, 83in. long. $1,745 £900

17th century oak centre table, 60¾in. wide. $1,740 £950

Early 18th century Continental walnut dining table on shaped legs, 6ft. long. $1,850 £950

Massive oak hall table. $1,980 £1,100

17th century oak refectory table, 77¾in. wide. $1,980 £1,100

17th century oak dining table, 78in. wide. $2,440 £1,250

Early 17th century pale oak refectory table, 96in. wide. $2,425 £1,250

Early 17th century oak dining table, 73½in. wide. $2,910 £1,500

George III oak dining table, 3ft.1in. wide, circa 1770. $2,990 £1,550

# REFECTORY TABLES

17th century South German refectory table, in oak, 84in. long. $3,705 £1,900

James I oak refectory table, 91in. x 31in. $3,780 £2,100

16th century oak refectory table, 6ft. long. $4,390 £2,250

17th century Florentine walnut refectory table, 7ft.6in. long.$4,385 £2,250

Elizabethan oak refectory table on six carved bulbous legs. $4,875 £2,500

17th century oak refectory table, with four plank top, 293cm. long. $8,490 £4,400

A massive early Georgian oak refectory table on six turned legs, with a plank top and drawer at either end, 28ft.8in. long. $8,775 £4,500

Elizabethan oak refectory table, 9ft. 11in. long. $10,800 £6,000

A Victorian mahogany table, with two drawers, on turned legs, 2ft.9in. wide. $65 £35

A 19th century mahogany half circle side table with drawer, on square tapered legs with spade feet, 3ft.8in. wide. $145 £75

Victorian carved oak side table with two drawers on shaped front legs with paw feet. $145 £75

Late 19th century French walnut side table on cabriole legs with scroll feet. $195 £100

A Continental walnut inlaid oblong table with drawer, on turned legs and club feet, 3ft. 1in. wide. $215 £110

George I oak side table with single drawer in the centre front and two large pear drop handles. $235 £120

19th century Chinese carved hardwood side table, 47in. wide. $240 £125

George III mahogany two-drawer side table with original ring handles, circa 1780. $285 £145

A rosewood side table with remarkable figuring of the wood, 55in. wide, circa 1840. $290 £150

Elm side table with original handles, circa 1790.
$390 £200

An early yew wood side table, with brass drop handles.
$390 £200

Mahogany three-drawer side table with cross-banded and matched feathered veneered top, circa 1770. $410 £210

George III mahogany side table on square tapering legs, 34in. high. $485 £250

Chippendale style mahogany oblong side table on cabriole legs and paw feet, 3ft. wide.
$485 £250

Queen Anne fruit-wood side table, circa 1710, 17in. high. $485 £250

19th century Chinese hardwood side table, 32 x 53½in.
$470 £260

Regency period brass inlaid rosewood side table. $680 £350

Oak side table cross-banded in mahogany, on cabriole legs, circa 1730. $730 £375

George II mahogany
side table, 4ft.5½in.
wide.     $825  £450

Early George III maho-
gany table, circa 1760,
2ft.6in. wide. $895  £460

George I walnut side
or dressing table with
three drawers, 2ft.9in.
wide.     $900  £500

18th century Dutch
marquetry tray top
silver table on shaped
legs with pad feet.
     $975  £500

North Italian gilt wood
side table with rectangu-
lar veined white marble
top, 1.30m. wide.
     $1,170  £600

Regency painted side
table with marble top,
3ft.10in. x 1ft.6in.
     $1,220  £625

Sheraton free stand-
ing side table in
satinwood, circa
1800. $1,265  £650

George III bowfronted
mahogany side table,
3ft.3in. wide, 1780.
     $1,170  £650

George II red walnut
side table with hip legs
and pad feet, fitted
with a frieze drawer.
     $1,265  £650

91

# SIDE TABLES

One of a pair of early 19th century serpentine front mahogany side tables in the Adam style.
$1,285  £660

A fine Irish Chippendale serving table of mahogany, heavily carved in the rococo manner. $1,520  £780

George II walnut side table, 2ft.6in. wide, circa 1730.
$1,440  £800

George II Irish mahogany side table, 4ft.10in. wide. $1,560  £800

One of a pair of late George III small D-shaped mahogany side tables, 2ft.3in. wide. $1,530  £850

18th century black lacquer side table with tray top, 2ft. 6in. wide.
$1,845  £950

One of a pair of Queen Anne side tables, circa 1710, 2ft.5in. wide.
$1,890  £1,050

One of a pair of George III mahogany side tables, 41½in. wide.
$1,980  £1,100

Late 18th century Dutch marquetry side table.
$2,340  £1,200

George I walnut side or dressing table, 2ft. 8in. wide.
$2,925  £1,500

One of a pair of George III gilt wood side tables with red marble tops, 35½in. wide.
$3,240  £1,800

One of a pair of mid 18th century South German gilt wood side tables, 59¼in. wide. $3,420  £1,900

Late George III satinwood side table, 57½in. wide.
$3,960  £2,200

George III satinwood marquetry semi-circular side table, 3ft.6¼in. wide.
$4,575  £2,500

One of a pair of Georgian bow-front side tables in mahogany.
$5,360  £2,750

Early 18th century gilt wood side table, 40in. wide.
$5,310  £2,950

One of a pair of gilt wood side tables in the manner of Wm. Kent, 55¾in. wide.
$5,760  £3,200

George III side table attributed to Thos. Chippendale with marquetry on a maple wood ground, on cabriole legs.
$37,050  £19,000

## SIDE TABLES
## PLATFORM BASE

Late Victorian walnut side table with under-shelf. $75 £40

A beautifully carved 19th century oak buffet with a green marble top, 60in. wide. $830 £425

18th century French walnut side table with two drawers and ormolu mounts. $975 £500

Regency rosewood pier table in the manner of Thomas Hope, 46½in. wide. $975 £500

Early 19th century Dutch marquetry side table, 2ft.6in. wide. $1,225 £680

George III satinwood breakfront side table, 2ft. wide. $2,745 £1,500

18th century marble topped Louis XVI marquetry table. $12,185 £6,250

Thomas Hope gilt pier table with black marble slab. $17,550 £9,000

One of a pair of Italian Pietra Dura tables. $18,050 £9,500

Sheraton breakfront mahogany serving table with line inlay. $1,170 £600

George III saintwood breakfront serving table, 71in. wide. $15,605 £800

Late George III fiddle-back mahogany serving table, 71¼in. wide. $1,800 £1,000

Important English gilt wood side table, circa 1815. $1,950 £1,000

Rare Louis XIV boulle side table, 4ft.10in. wide. $8,775 £4,500

One of a pair of side tables by Robert Adam, circa 1770, 1.56m. wide. $17,640 £9,800

One of a pair of English late 18th century tables attributed to John Linnell, in gilt wood, with a marble top. $19,500 £10,000

Marquetry curved side table designed by Chippendale. $19,500 £10,000

One of a pair of gilt wood side tables. $18,000 £10,000

## SIDE TABLES
## STRETCHER BASE

Victorian walnut
side table, circa
1890.
$145  £75

18th century oak
side table, with a
carved frieze, 40in.
wide.  $245  £125

An 18th century
oak side table with
cross stretchers,
30½in. wide.
$310  £160

English oak side
table, 3ft. wide,
late 17th century.
$485  £250

Highly carved 19th
century hardwood
side table.
$560  £300

17th century oak side
table, 33in. long, 23in.
wide, 28in. high.
$680  £350

Small 17th century
oak side table in
excellent condition.
$830  £425

Late George III yew
and rosewood table.
$820  £440

Late 17th century
oak side table, 33in.
wide.    $890  £460

19th century boulle
side table with
ormolu mounts.
$1,055 £540

A William and Mary olive
wood side table, the oblong
top oyster veneered and
with pearwood geometric
inlays, 37in. wide.
$1,100 £565

Dutch small marquetry
inlaid side table, 2ft.
7½in. wide, circa 1680.
$1,065 £580

Side table of ivory
inlaid ebony, 39in.
wide.$1,080 £600

18th century Italian
gilt wood side table,
65½in. wide.
$1,100 £600

Late 18th century
mahogany silver
table of Chinese
Chippendale design,
3ft. x 1ft.11½in.
$1,170 £600

Mid 17th century
North Italian gilt
wood side table.
$1,265 £650

A good William and
Mary walnut side
table with marquetry
decoration.
$1,655 £850

One of a pair of
Regency simulated
rosewood side
tables with marble
tops. $1,705 £875

## SIDE TABLES
## STRETCHER BASE

William and Mary period walnut side table decorated with seaweed marquetry panels.
$1,950 £1,000

Late 17th century oak side table, 49½in. wide.
$1,830 £1,000

18th century Chinese black lacquer side table.
$1,990 £1,020

Late 17th century oak side table.
$2,400 £1,250

Early 17th century James I oak side table, 6ft.6in. long.
$2,800 £1,450

17th century Spanish walnut side table, 46in. wide.
$3,010 £1,550

17th century Dutch mother-of-pearl and lacquered side table, 48in. wide.
$4,875 £2,500

Giltwood side table, circa 1720, 62in. wide, possibly German. $4,760 £2,600

French Regency period side table by Nicolas-Pierre Severin.
$39,000 £20,000

An Edwardian satin-
wood sofa table.
$680  £350

Mahogany and satin-
wood banded sofa
table, 1.60m. x 64cm.
extended. $780  £400

Early 19th century
rosewood and brass
inlaid sofa table,
1.38m. x 39cm.
$1,365  £700

George III mahogany
sofa table, with origi-
nal wooden pulls,
having brass-tipped
feet. $1,755  £900

George III mahogany
sofa table with splayed
legs, 59in. long when
open, 35in. wide, 26in.
high.  $1,950  £1,000

Sheraton satinwood
sofa table crossban-
ded with rosewood
and inlaid with box-
wood and ebony
stringing, circa 1800.
$2,630  £1,350

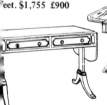

Regency sofa table,
5ft. x 2ft., in
figured rosewood.
$3,315  £1,700

Late 18th century
coromandel wood
sofa table cross-
banded with satin-
wood. $3,410  £1,750

Regency satinwood
and rosewood ban-
ded sofa table.
$6,695  £3,600

# SOFA TABLES
## CENTRAL COLUMN

William IV rosewood sofa table, 88cm. wide.    $600 £310

Early 19th century mahogany sofa table on a platform base with paw feet.    $875 £450

A Regency mahogany sofa table, decorated with coromandel wood crossbanding, 4ft.8in. fully extended.    $875 £450

Regency rosewood sofa table on a platform base with reeded legs.    $1,070 £550

Good quality Regency, rosewood sofa table.    $1,170 £600

George III mahogany sofa table on reeded legs, 36in. wide.    $1,220 £625

William IV mahogany sofa table, on lyre support, with ormolu mounts, 30in. high, 37in. wide, 27in. deep.    $1,610 £825

A Regency brass inlaid sofa table on a platform base with claw feet.    $1,640 £840

Regency rosewood sofa table inlaid with brass lines.    $1,530 £850

Regency mahogany sofa table on pedestal supports with brass castors, 152 x 59cm. $975 £500

Regency period mahogany crossbanded sofa table. $975 £500

A Regency period calamanderwood sofa table, with boxwood string inlay. $2,340 £1,200

An elegant, late 18th century mahogany sofa table. $2,340 £1,200

Early 19th century George III pale mahogany sofa table, 62½in. wide, open. $2,730 £1,400

Good Regency brass inlaid rosewood sofa table, 3ft.2in. wide. $2,730 £1,400

Regency partridge wood sofa table, inlaid and crossbanded, supported on slender curving legs. $3,300 £1,650

Regency rosewood sofa table with split top. $4,095 £2,100

A fine rosewood sofa table, 5ft. overall. $6,240 £3,200

A small sofa table in mahogany with ebony inlay, circa 1840. $350 £180

Small rosewood sofa table, 39½in. wide, 1850's. $580 £300

A mahogany inlaid sofa table with two folding leaves and a drawer, 2ft 4in. x 1ft.4in. $680 £350

Mahogany sofa table with two drawers, top 30 x 36in., circa 1850. $730 £375

A mid 19th century sofa table in faded mahogany, the top 21in. x 33in. with flaps raised. $730 £375

19th century mahogany inlaid sofa table, with a shell motif in the centre. $750 £385

Edwardian Sheraton style satinwood inlaid sofa table with 'D' shaped leaves, 4ft. 7in. wide overall.$925 £475

William IV mahogany sofa table, 5ft.2in. wide, circa 1830. $935 £520

Regency rosewood and parcel gilt sofa table, 53½in. wide, open. $990 £550

Regency simulated
rosewood sofa table,
61¾in. wide.
$1,350  £750

Regency rosewood
sofa table with bob-
bin twist supports
and ebony banding.
$1,560  £800

18th century drop-
leaf sofa table, deco-
rated overall with
marquetry flowers.
$1,990  £1,020

A Regency period
faded rosewood
sofa table with fine
brass mounts.
$2,145  £1,100

A Regency rosewood,
lyre ended sofa table,
the top crossbanded
in the same wood,
circa 1810.
$2,145  £1,100

Regency rosewood
sofa table.
$3,315  £1,700

Regency rosewood
sofa table banded
with satinwood,
1.37m. extended.
$5,360  £2,750

Regency brass inlaid
sofa table, 5ft. wide,
open. $5,125  £2,800

Fine Regency rose-
wood sofa table,
67½in. wide, exten-
ded. $6,840  £3,600

Georgian mahogany and parcel gilt sofa table, 65in. wide.
$975 £500

Late Regency period rosewood sofa table on twist supports.
$1,080 £540

A George IV rosewood sofa table, on platform base with splay feet and brass castors, 44in. wide.
$1,070 £550

Regency rosewood sofa table, 39in. wide.
$1,120 £575

An early 19th century mahogany sofa table.
$1,460 £750

Attractive Regency rosewood sofa table.
$1,550 £800

Regency rosewood sofa table.
$1,655 £850

Regency period rosewood sofa table with brass string inlay and crossbanded in satinwood. $1,950 £1,000

Regency calamander-wood sofa table with two flap top, 59in. wide. $4,500 £2,500

Bamboo plant stand with tiled top, circa 1900.    $75  £40

An early Victorian mahogany circular lamp table, on polygonal stems. $85  £45

Chinese carved padouk wood jardiniere stand, 2ft. high.  $165  £85

Louis Philippe period gueridon table in kingwood with ormolu mounts and rose marble top.       $585  £300

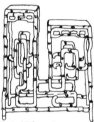

Late 19th century rosewood etagere with two tops.      $730  £375

An Italian ebonised blackamoor table, 34in. high, 26in. diam.  $730  £375

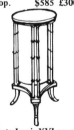

Late Louis XVI ormolu and amboyna gueridon, 14½in. diam.
        $3,295  £1,800

One of a pair of George III mahogany torcheres, 38¾in. high.
        $3,240  £1,800

Mid 19th century French gilt metal gueridon table, inset with Sevres plaques, signed S. Simonnen, 31in. diam.  $9,750  £5,000

# SUTHERLAND TABLES

Small Victorian ebonised Sutherland table, 1ft.9in. wide. $60 £30

Mahogany Sutherland tea table with two drop-leaves, 2ft.3in. wide. $85 £45

Small Edwardian inlaid mahogany Sutherland table with half round flaps. $105 £55

A small, late 19th century mahogany Sutherland table, with a crossbanded top. $115 £60

A rosewood inlaid oblong two-tier table with folding leaves and satinwood banded borders, 2ft. wide. $125 £65

A small walnut Sutherland tea table with ebonised borders. $135 £70

Victorian mahogany Sutherland table with shaped flaps, on a turned underframe. $145 £75

Mahogany inlaid and satinwood banded Sutherland tea table on turned legs, 2ft. wide. $155 £80

Victorian walnut Sutherland table on turned legs, 76cm. wide. $155 £80

A rosewood inlaid Sutherland tea table, with two folding leaves, standing on turned legs, 2ft. wide. $165 £85

Victorian walnut Sutherland table on a turned underframe. $165 £85

Victorian mahogany Sutherland table, 1m. wide. $195 £100

Victorian rosewood Sutherland table on twist supports. $215 £110

Walnut Sutherland table, 22¼in., circa 1880. $225 £120

Victorian walnut oval shaped Sutherland table, 3ft.1in. wide. $245 £125

Early Victorian burr walnut Sutherland table with oval flaps and cabriole leg supports. $290 £150

A nicely figured burr walnut Sutherland table, circa 1860, 41½in. wide. $370 £200

Sutherland table in mahogany with brass inlay. $540 £300

107

# TRIANGULAR TOP TABLES

Edwardian folding top card table in walnut. $125 £65

A late 18th century oak triangular table with three folding leaves, on turned legs. $165 £85

A Victorian carved oak triangular table with folding leaf on a gateleg support, 2ft.9in. wide. $165 £85

Late 18th century Dutch walnut and marquetry inlaid triangular shaped folding table, 95cm. wide. $875 £450

Rare yew wood envelope table with flap supported by a loper, circa 1730. $1,415 £725

16th century English oak triangular envelope table, 69cm. wide. $3,410 £1,750

# WAKES TABLES

A fine quality late 18th century Irish Wakes table in cherrywood. $1,265 £650

A good George III mahogany Wakes table, on square legs. $1,460 £750

A large mid 18th century Irish Wakes table in mahogany. $2,925 £1,500

19th century mahogany work table, the hinged box top with panel of red and gold lacquer, 1ft.9in. wide. $95 £50

Late 19th century inlaid mahogany work table with a rising top, dummy drawer and real drawer. $125 £65

19th century mahogany work table with hinged box top, dummy drawer and real drawer, 1ft. 11in. wide. $155 £80

Mid 19th century mahogany Pembroke style work table on square tapering legs.$165 £85

Edwardian inlaid mahogany work table with hinged flaps. $165 £85

George III amboyna work table, 40cm. wide. $195 £100

Late 18th century rosewood veneered work table, 45cm. wide. $235 £120

Early 19th century mahogany sewing table on fine turned legs, with fitted top drawer. $275 £140

Early 19th century inlaid and satinwood banded oblong work table on square tapered legs, 52cm. wide. $290 £150

# WORK/SEWING TABLES

**George III mahogany work table with flaps, supported on turned legs with castors.**
$300 £155

**Regency period mahogany sewing table with ebony inlay and fluted tapering legs.** $340 £175

**19th century marquetry work table on fine turned legs.**
$390 £200

**Late 18th century mahogany work table on fine fluted legs.** $535 £275

**A French, serpentine shaped ebony and red boulle work table, of Louis XV design standing on cabriole legs.** $730 £375

**Victorian burr walnut and marquetry work table, 22in. high.**
$1,055 £540

**Early 19th century Regency penwork sewing table, 20in. wide.** $1,040 £540

**19th century French work table in kingwood and mahogany with ormolu decoration.** $1,365 £700

**A satinwood worktable, circa 1790, 2ft.5¾in. high, 1ft. 6in. wide.**
$1,460 £750

## CENTRAL COLUMN

## WORK/SEWING TABLES

Late Victorian mahogany sewing table with two drawers on a turned central column and platform base.
$145 £75

A mahogany work table with hinged top, on pillar and fluted claw, with brass paw terminals.
$155 £80

Early 19th century drop-leaf mahogany sewing table with one real and one dummy drawer.
$275 £140

A Victorian walnut and inlaid oblong work table with hinged top, on pillar and claw, 19½in. wide.
$290 £150

Early Victorian work table with flaps, on a turned central column with a shaped platform base.
$310 £155

Victorian mahogany work table with drawer and well, on central column with shaped base.
$310 £160

An early Victorian sewing table with drop flaps and a U-shaped centre support.
$350 £180

19th century octagonal top rosewood work table on a platform base with scroll feet.
$350 £180

Early 19th century work table on pedestal base.
$360 £185

111

## WORK/SEWING TABLES
### CENTRAL COLUMN

19th century pollard elm work table with brass claw castors. $360 £185

Regency rosewood lady's work table with shaped platform base. $360 £185

Fine quality Victorian papier mache work table with fitted interior. $460 £235

A mahogany work table with parquetry worked top, circa 1830, 27 x 19in. $535 £275

Late Regency walnut and rosewood work table inlaid with brass, copper and mother-of-pearl, 21in. wide. $545 £280

Regency octagonal satinwood work table. $565 £290

Regency mahogany work table with drop flaps and splay feet with brass castors. $635 £325

A fine Victorian papier mache work table with gilt decoration. $635 £325

Regency mahogany work table, 21½in. $635 £325

A fine Regency work table with a fitted drawer, in faded mahogany. $720 £370

Regency work table on claw feet. $720 £370

Regency period parquetry work table with elaborate toes and castors. $730 £375

Regency brass inlaid rosewood sewing table. $780 £400

An early 19th century work table with a fitted interior and silk covered work basket. $830 £425

Good Regency period work table veneered in amboyna. $830 £425

Unusual Charles X rosewood sewing table on down-curved legs, 1ft. 2in. diam. $925 £475

Faded rosewood work table with sewing compartments, circa 1830. $975 £500

19th century Biedermeier ebonised and parcel gilt globe work table, 96cm. high. $2,535 £1,300

Victorian mahogany work box with drawer. $175 £90

Stripped pine sewing table with fitted interior and original ivory escutcheon and knobs. $245 £125

A fine 19th century Sheraton style octagonal work table. $275 £140

Victorian inlaid walnut work table with folding top. $300 £155

19th century black export lacquer work table decorated with gilt chinoiserie scenes, 70cm. wide. $310 £160

Late Regency burr walnut and oak work table with one dummy and two real drawers. $310 £160

19th century English mahogany work table with a fitted drawer, circa 1850. $390 £200

William IV mahogany sewing table, 24in. wide. $390 £200

Mid 19th century Anglo-Indian padouk work table with crisply carved decoration. $440 £225

Victorian papier mache work box decorated with mother-of-pearl.
$485 £250

A superb quality Victorian rosewood sewing table on a stretcher base with cabriole legs.
$555 £285

Fine quality work table in mahogany with brass string inlay, 14in. square, 30in. high, circa 1810. $635 £325

19th century marquetry work table with ormolu embellishments, 20in. wide. $780 £400

Early 19th century mahogany work table with ormolu enrichments.
$780 £400

A fine Regency period satinwood work table on a stretcher base, with lyre supports.
$830 £425

Early 19th century satinwood work table. $875 £450

Early Victorian black lacquered papier mache work table, 20in. wide.
$895 £460

Regency period work table with boxwood string inlay.
$925 £475

## WORK/SEWING TABLES
## STRETCHER BASE

A Regency sewing table with a rising screen and adjustable reading slope. $935 £480

Georgian rosewood sewing table with two drawers and sewing compartment, the base with brass toe castors, circa 1820. $945 £485

Good, George III, parquetry sewing and writing table, 1ft.11in. wide. $1,025 £525

Late 18th century satinwood work table with painted decoration. $1,460 £750

A Regency kingwood and rosewood work table, with small sabre legs and claw feet. $1,560 £800

Regency tortoiseshell and rosewood sewing table. $1,620 £840

Lady's tulipwood work table in the Sheraton style with purplewood marquetry, 1ft.10¼in. wide. $2,435 £1,250

Rare mid 19th century French work box in satinwood and kingwood, 34in. high. $2,925 £1,500

Regency mahogany reading and work table, with an adjustable writing slide, a work cabinet below. $3,315 £1,700

116

Edwardian mahogany
writing table with in-
set leather top and
turned legs. $50 £25

Victorian mahogany
writing table on
turned legs. $60 £30

Late 19th century
oak writing table
with inset leather
top. $160 £85

20th century repro-
duction walnut
writing table on
cabriole legs, 42in.
wide. $195 £100

A fine writing table, the
top inset with green
tooled leather with a
stationery cupboard,
2ft.6in. wide.$195 £100

19th century serpen-
tine table in the French
manner with ormolu
mounts and centre
drawer. $265 £135

William IV mahogany
writing table with gold
leather top, 42 x 23in.
$275 £140

Early Victorian writing
table with leather lined
top, on reeded legs.
$275 £140

Fruitwood writing
table with drawer,
36 x 24½in., circa
1820. $310 £160

# WRITING TABLES

Good Georgian mahogany writing table with original handles and green leather top. Top size 36 x 23in., circa 1800.    $440 £225

19th century Burmese padouk wood writing table.    $525 £270

Late 17th century oak writing table, the three drawers to the frieze crossbanded with walnut, 2ft. wide.
$525 £270

Useful mahogany table with centre turnover panel, 42in. wide, circa 1820.    $635 £325

Oak writing table by Gordon Russell, 48¼in. long.    $650 £360

Late 18th century mahogany writing table with fretwork decoration and faded green leather top, 36in. wide.  $730 £375

19th century figured walnut writing table of kidney shape standing on ormolu mounted cabriole legs.  $780 £400

Unusual early 19th century mahogany tutor's desk.
$830 £425

Elegant library table with concave front, reeded legs and leather top, 53in. wide, circa 1850. $830 £425

Mid 18th century drop-leaf writing table, 3ft.6in. wide. $860 £440

20th century mahogany writing table, with galleried top, 36in. wide. $1,005 £520

Edwards and Roberts walnut writing desk, circa 1860, on carved legs. $1,120 £575

Italian walnut writing or dressing table, circa 1780, 3ft.5in. wide. $1,115 £620

Edwardian satinwood lady's breakfront writing desk, 3ft.6in. wide. $1,220 £625

Sheraton style mahogany writing table, circa 1800. $1,265 £650

19th century French walnut bureau de dame. $1,475 £820

Louis XV kingwood and marquetry table a ecrire, 17½in. wide. $1,950 £1,000

Ormolu mounted Louis XVI style writing table on tapering legs with brass castors. $1,950 £1,000

# WRITING TABLES

French kingwood
and marquetry
writing table in the
Louis Quinze style.
$2,340 £1,200

Italian walnut table
with writing slide
and two drawers.
$2,520 £1,400

19th century kingwood
writing table decorated
with ormolu and Sevres
plaques, 33in. wide.
$2,730 £1,400

Louis XVI marquetry
writing table on
square tapering legs,
1ft.4in. wide.
$3,120 £1,600

19th century king-
wood writing table,
41½in. wide.
$4,875 £2,500

18th century kingwood
parquetry writing table,
with a serpentine top
and tapering cabriole
legs, 20in. wide.
$8,285 £4,250

French kingwood and
tulipwood writing
table with ormolu
mounts, 1.12m. wide.
$12,675 £6,500

Matching mahogany
chair and bureau by
Louis Majorelle.
$44,470 £24,705

Rare small writing
table signed de
Joseph.
$226,485 £116,145

Louis Philippe king-
wood parquetry
bureau plat, 39½in.
x 23½in. $715 £370

Louis XVI style maho-
gany kneehole bureau
plat with brass mounts,
borders and gallery,
148cm. wide.
$1,265 £650

Small bureau plat
with ormolu mounts
and inlaid in rare tim-
bers, 5ft.1in. wide.
$1,850 £950

Early 18th century style
French serpentine shaped
bureau plat in tulip and
kingwood, 2ft.10in. wide.
$4,320 £2,400

Louis XVI boulle small
bureau plat with moul-
ded brass border, 3ft.
5in. wide.
$7,800 £4,000

Louis XV ormolu moun-
ted tulipwood bureau
plat, top inset with tooled
leather, 3ft.10in. wide.
$11,700 £6,000

Louis XVI mahogany
marquetry bureau
plat by J. H. Reisener.
$58,500 £30,000

Louis XV period
bureau plat and car-
tonnier, by Jean-
Francois Dubut,
1.28m. long.
$136,500 £70,000

Louis XVI ormolu moun-
ted ebony bureau plat
and cartonnier, surmoun-
ted by a clock signed by
Robin Paris.
$468,000 £240,000

A lady's Sheraton mahogany inlaid writing table, on turned, fluted legs and cross stretchers, 1ft.10½in. wide.
$195 £100

Edwardian inlaid mahogany and satinwood banded oblong writing table on square tapered legs, 60cm. wide. $245 £125

A Victorian ebonised and satinwood inlaid writing table of Louis XVI design with drawers in frieze and inset with china plaques. $310 £160

William and Mary oak writing table.
$485 £250

Late 19th century rosewood writing table with serpentine front.
$585 £300

Jacobean oak writing table with two drawers, on a stretcher base.
$780 £400

A George III Cuban mahogany library table, 4ft.6in.
$1,170 £600

A nicely proportioned carved gilt wood library table, circa 1830.
$2,925 £1,500

19th century boulle writing table.
$3,510 £1,800

Victorian inlaid mahogany and rosewood banded writing table, with spiral end supports, 102cm. wide. $275 £140

A good quality Victorian rosewood writing table. $440 £225

A Victorian mahogany writing table with green leather top, 38in. wide. $505 £260

Early Victorian mahogany library table with an extensively inlaid rectangular top, 52½in. x 19in. $780 £400

Library table with finely marked rosewood veneers, 58in. long, circa 1840. $830 £425

George III mahogany writing table with drawer, on splay feet with brass castors. $1,025 £525

Unusual Regency seaweed marquetry writing table, 37¼in. wide. $1,520 £780

One of a pair of William IV yew and pollard yew writing tables, 60in. wide. $2,700 £1,500

Regency mahogany writing table, 53½in. wide. $3,570 £1,850

123

# INDEX

Accounting 63
Adjustable Top 8
Altar 63
Architects' 8
Art Furniture 70
Artist's 8

Bedside 63
Biedermeier 17, 113
Bijouterie 49
Blackamoor 105
Boardroom 39
Book Trolley 84
Boudoir 51
Breakfast/Supper 9, 41 - 46, 77
Buffet 85, 94
Butler, E. 57
Bureau De Dame 119
Bureau Plat 121
B.V.R.B. 71

Card And Tea 10 - 21, 27, 64, 106 - 108
Carlton House 22
Cartonnier 121
Central Column 25, 26, 100, 111 - 113
Central Column, Cabriole Leg 10, 41
Central Column, Platform Base 11, 42, 43
Central Column, Splay Feet 12
Central Column, Splay Feet, Rectangular Top 46
Central Column, Splay Feet, Round Top 44, 45
Centre 23 - 30, 67, 86, 87
Chess Top 31, 32
China Plaques 28, 122

Coffee 28, 65
Collman, L.W. 24
Concertina Action 18, 19
Consol 33 - 35
Consol Desserte 35
Corner 36
Cottage 52
Crace 21, 67
Credence 36
Cricket 37

D'Accoucher 63
'D' End 13, 39, 47
'D' End Flaps 78, 79, 102
Desk 22, 118, 119
Desky, Donald 35
Detachable Leaf 9
Dining 9, 38 - 48, 50, 52, 53, 58, 85, 87
Display 49
Domino 73
Draughtsman's 84
Draw-Leaf 50
Dressing 51, 91, 93, 119
Drinking 39
Drinking Cabinet 63
Drop-Flap 79, 112
Drop-Leaf 52, 53, 59, 81, 82, 106, 111, 119
Drum 54, 55
Dubut, Jean-Francois 121
Dumb Waiter 70
Dummy Drawer 23, 109, 111

Easel 84
Edwards And Roberts 119

Effect 73
Envelope 14, 108
Etagere 70, 71, 105
Extending 40, 47

Folding Stand 65
Four Pillar 16

Galle 64
Gallery Top 66
Games 11, 17, 18, 31, 32, 56, 57, 64
Gateleg 53, 58 - 61, 108
Gillow 82
Gueridon 69, 105
Gypsy 73

Half Round 15, 106
Half Round Flaps 80, 81
Hall 62, 87
Harlequin 82
Hexagonal 71
High Stretcher 101
Hunting 43, 53

Irish Wakes 108

Jardiniere 63, 105
Joass, J.J. 38
Johnson, Thomas 19
Joseph, De 120

Kent, Wm. 93

Lacquered Top 19, 27, 67, 70, 74
Lady's 111, 119, 122
Lamp 105

Library 54, 55, 118, 122
Linnell, John 95
Loo 41, 43, 44
Low 23
Low Stretcher 102, 103

Mackintosh, Charles Rennie 73
Majorelle, Louis 120
Maple & Co. 22
Mirror Panels 69
Mirror Top 72
Miscellaneous 63
Mouseman 85
Multiple Column 16, 104
Multiple Leg 17

Naylor, Rowland 75
Nest 64

Occasional 65-77, 79, 80
Octagonal top 67

Paris, Robin 121
Pay 28, 63
Pedestal 67, 69, 74, 77
Pedestal Chest 73
Pembroke 31, 78 - 83, 109
Phyle, Duncan 40
Pier 34, 94
Platform Base 94
Platform Base, Rectangular Top 68
Platform Base, Round Top 69
Poudreuse 51
Protruding Corners 18
Pub 73

Quartetto 64

Reading 84, 116
Rectangular Flaps 82
Rectangular Top 19
Refectory 85 - 88
Reisener, J.H. 35, 121
Rent 55, 67
Reversible Top 56
Revolving Top 54
Rhulmann, Emile-Jacques 28, 51
Rising Top 109
Russell, Gordon 118
RVLC JME 73

Salon 25, 70
Screen 116
Serpentine Front 20
Serving 92, 95
Set 64
Settle 63
Severin, Nicolas-Pierre 98
Sevres Plaques 105, 120
Sewing 31, 109 - 116
Shaped Flaps 83, 106
Shaped Top 21
Shelf Base 70, 71
SHL 36
Showcase 49
Side 52, 69, 89 - 98
Silver 91, 97
Simonnen, S. 105
Six Legs 95
Slide 23, 116, 120
Sofa 99 - 104
Specimen 49
Spider Leg 52
Stand 84, 105
Stationery Cupboard 117
Strahan & Co., Robert 54

Stretcher Base 27, 28, 31, 72, 96 - 98,
    114 - 116, 122
Supper/Breakfast 9, 41 - 46, 77
Surprise 63
Sutherland 106, 107

Table a Cafe 71
Tahn of Paris 51
Tambour Cabinet 36
Tavern 86
Tea and Card 10 - 21, 27, 64, 106 -
    108
Telescopic 38, 39
Three Legs 73
Three Pillar 48
Toilet 51
Torchere 105
Tray Top 76, 91, 92
Trestle Base 30, 72, 123
Triangular Top 108
Tricoteuse 71
Triple Fold Top 17
Tripod Base, Rectangular Top 74
Tripod Base, Round Top 75
Tripod Base, Shaped Top 76, 77
Tunbridge Ware 32
Tutor's Desk 118
Two Pillar 47
Two-Tier 67, 70, 73, 106

Wakes 108
Well 53
Wine 29, 74
Work 31, 32, 109 - 116
Work Box 115
Writing 22, 32, 79, 117 - 123
Writing Slide 116, 120